The World of Willa Cather

The front endpaper is from an old print of Red Cloud in 1880. Represented are: (1) Silas Garber residence, site of original stockade and setting for *A Lost Lady*; (2) Cather home, used in *My Ántonia, Song of the Lark* and "Old Mrs. Harris"; (3) Miner home, the "Harling" place in *My Ántonia*; orchard is mentioned in *Lucy Gayheart*; (4) site of Wiener house, the "Rosen" home in "Old Mrs. Harris"; (5) Court House, mentioned in *Song of the Lark* and *One of Ours*; (6) Crooked Creek, described in *Song of the Lark* and *A Lost Lady*; (7) Methodist Church, described in *Song of the Lark* as facing the Court House; (8) Uncle Will Jackson's cottonwood grove, described in *Song of the Lark*; (9) road to the depot settlement of *Song of the Lark*; (10) Burlington and Missouri Railroad, described in *My Ántonia, One of Ours*, "The Sculptor's Funeral," etc.; (11) Boy's Home Hotel, the "Gardener House" of *My Ántonia*; (12) Miner Brothers' Store of *O Pioneers* and *My Ántonia*; (13) the Republican River, appearing in almost all Miss Cather's Nebraska books and stories. The back endpaper is from an old woodcut of Webster Street.

STRAHORN LIBRARY
COLLEGE OF IDAHO

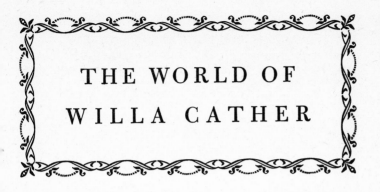

THE WORLD OF WILLA CATHER

By Mildred R. Bennett

ILLUSTRATED WITH PHOTOGRAPHS AND DRAWINGS

Dodd, Mead & Company • *New York*

PUBLISHED FEBRUARY, 1951

SECOND PRINTING MARCH, 1951

THIRD PRINTING MARCH, 1951

FOURTH PRINTING MAY, 1951

For Bert Rhoads and Will Bennett

~Acknowledgments

To THE FOLLOWING PEOPLE of Webster County I am indebted: Vernon Walters who has patiently reproduced old prints; Mrs. Ray Wilson, daughter of Mr. and Mrs. Henry Lambrecht; Mrs. Telia Erickson, daughter of Hans Skjelver; Mrs. Hilda Peterson; Mrs. R. I. Cooper; Wilella Paine Wilson, daughter of Alverna Cather Paine and Carrie Cather Lindgren, daughter of George Cather, both of whom loaned me family photographs; Mrs. Anna Pavelka and her daughter Elizabeth Boyd; Mr. and Mrs. Henry Lambrecht, Lydia and Pauline Lambrecht and Clara Lambrecht Lovejoy —all children of Mr. and Mrs. Fred Lambrecht; Mr. and Mrs. Hugh Miner (Retta Ayres, daughter of Jennie Cather Ayres); Mrs. Jennie Reiher, daughter of Mr. and Mrs. Hugh Miner; Mary Miner Creighton who was Willa's first friend in Red Cloud; Barbara Newhouse Phares; Mrs. Louise Ketchum, daughter of the Reverend Mr. Bates; L. L. Peirce; Mrs. D. B. Burden, daughter-in-law of Jim Burden; Mrs. Harvey

Rickerson; Walter B. Smith, owner and editor of "The Commercial Advertiser," who gave me free access to the files of old Red Cloud papers.

I wish to thank Miss Mariel Gere and Mrs. John Almy for helping me reconstruct the Willa of University days, and Miss Flora Bullock for her excellent work on Cather bibliography of the Lincoln years. I wish to thank Grant Reynard for his letters; Blanche Cather Ray, daughter of George Cather, for information from the Cather family records; Boris Hambourg of Toronto, Canada for information about his brother, Jan; G. W. Gerwig and George Seibel of Pittsburgh for their letters.

The following persons helped me obtain material and verify data: Kate Field and Eunice Willis of the University of Nebraska Registrar's office; Oscar F. Humble, Director of Examining Boards, State of Nebraska; Mrs. Sumner Willard, The Wilbur Library, University of Vermont, Burlington, Vt.; Mrs. Edward Cushing writing for Olive Fremsted; Mrs. Mabel Dodge Luhan of Taos, New Mexico; Reginald L. Cook, Director of the Bread Loaf School of English, Middlebury, Vt.; Rose Demorest of the Pennsylvania Room, Carnegie Library, Pittsburgh; Mrs. Estel Cheever, Los Angeles; Mrs. Althea Seamark, librarian at the "Lincoln State Journal"; Mrs. Bertha Fisher of the Auld Library, Red Cloud; Floyd R. Meyer of the University of Nebraska

Acknowledgments

Library; James C. Olson, president of the Nebraska State Historical Society; Sister Rose Margaret, librarian at Loretto Heights Girls' School, Denver; Sister M. Matilda, Loretto Motherhouse, Nerinx, Kentucky; the priests at both St. Thomas Seminary and Holy Ghost Church in Denver; M. Jean Malyé, Le Président Directeur général, Les Belles Lettres, Paris; La Société des Amis de la Bibliothèque Nationale, Paris; Mrs. Grace Standeven of Omaha, Dr. E. N. Dick of Lincoln, John Clopine, Jr., of Washington, D. C.; Frank Magel of the Book-of-the-Month Club, Mrs. Harvey Newbranch of Omaha, Mrs. J. H. Grosvenor of Aurora, Judge D. M. Vinsonhaler of Omaha; Miss Eleanor Hinman and Miss Anne Gilham of Lincoln. I also wish to mention the unpublished master's thesis on the Nebraska sources of Cather material by Joan Ballard of the University of California at Los Angeles.

My appreciation goes to Dr. L. C. Wimberly of the University of Nebraska for his encouragement; to Dorothy Canfield Fisher for her letters and her suggestions; to Robert Frost for his interest; to Miss Elsie Cather for her checking and rechecking of the facts in the manuscript and for her invaluable information; and to David E. Scherman for his editorial work.

Special credit should go to two people: Dr. L. V. Jacks of Creighton University, Omaha who conducts the Omaha Writers' Conference, for suggesting this

Acknowledgments

book and following up with helpful criticisms and information; and Carrie Miner Sherwood who has been my constant helper. For a number of years she has collected information about Miss Cather. From about 1915 on, Miss Cather sent Mrs. Sherwood all sorts of material, saying, "I know you have a large attic and you won't mind keeping this for me." This unusual collection has given me information which I could not have otherwise obtained. Mrs. Sherwood, herself, has driven all over the county with me to visit the scenes and people of the Cather books. She has read and helped revise every word of this manuscript. Without her the book could never have been written.

To Dr. W. K. Bennett, Mary Etta Busch and my son Bill: Thank you for your patience and cooperation.

MILDRED R. BENNETT

FOREWORD

A book is made with one's own flesh and blood of years . . . it is cremated youth. It is all yours—no one gave it to you.
—WILLA CATHER, Omaha, 1921

A LITERARY CRITIC once observed that Willa Sibert Cather had first to "overcome the Nebraska in her" to achieve success as the author of *O Pioneers, My Án-tonia* and a dozen other books, as one of America's first-rank novelists.

Hardly any statement could have been farther from the truth. It was the "Nebraska in her"—her childhood among the many-tongued pioneers and homesteaders of Webster and Franklin Counties, her roamings on pony-back over the tough long prairie grass, and her education, or revulsion to it, in a bustling, wooden-sidewalked prairie town—it was all this that left its indelible mark on almost everything she wrote in later years. And it was this that caused her to complain, in those later years of worldwide fame, that Nebraska—"that country—was the happiness and the curse" of her life.

Her mixed feelings toward this world of bleak, wild prairie, where she lived from 1883 to 1896, her love and hatred of it, were the feelings of a sensitive child to a parent: she blessed what it gave her, in life-long friendships, in emotional release, and, in a more material sense, in subject-matter for her greatest writing; she hated it for the hold it had on her, for the acute longing she felt for it wherever in the world she happened to find herself. Employ it she did, magnificently; overcome it, never.

Not that Willa Cather was in any sense a provincial. From Sara Orne Jewett she learned early in her career that "to write about the parish one must know the world." She began to satisfy her curiosity about the world from childhood on, but of her writing she once said that the only part of life that made a real impression on her imagination and emotion was what happened to her before the age of twenty.

If one bridles at this false assumption that Willa Cather had to get Nebraska out of her system, there is still a mystery to be explained—how did anyone so closely tied to a Nebraska-prairie childhood develop such a worldliness of outlook and style and genius for expression that it broke into print with wide critical acclaim even before she had finished her term at the University?

The answer probably lies in the little-realized fact

that Nebraska frontier life of the 1880's, while rugged in the extreme, was far from the notion of barren, cultureless hickdom that the vaudeville comedian has tried so hard to make popular. The countryside, in particular the countryside around Red Cloud, Willa's childhood home, was an intellectual melting pot of Bohemian, Russian, German, French, Swedish and Norwegian first-generation immigrant pioneers, to which were added the cultures of New England and the Cathers' own gracious Virginia. The pioneers who came to seek their fortune on the inhospitable new land—some to perish in the attempt from sheer loneliness, like gentle Bohemian Papa Shimerda of *My Ántonia*—were by no means the hard-riding, gun-toting adventurers of the Western films. Musicians, botanists, world-traveled linguists and frustrated painters were Willa's childhood neighbors as often as the tireless farmers of the outlying lands. The railroad that built Red Cloud disgorged daily traveling troupes of actors who had come from the civilized East and voyagers from the Orient (via California) who were going there.

The stimulating influence of this conglomeration is still felt today, in spite of the success-complacency of the second and third generations that Willa Cather so deplored in later years, and from which she fled. But it was there in full strength when she was a child, and she soaked it up (as Mark Twain earlier soaked up the culture of the Missouri country to the south) rejecting what she considered ignoble or impermanent, accepting what she thought was the real frontier.

How this part of America grew up with Willa Cather, and who those friends, relations and acquaintances were that made such an enduring emotional impression on her life and writing this book will try to describe.

Red Cloud, Nebraska, 1950.

CONTENTS

Contents

DRAMA

ILLUSTRATIONS

Illustrations

The World of Willa Cather

THE FAMILY

I

"O Pioneers"

WHEN WILLA CATHER, daughter of a gentleman sheep-rancher and his patrician Virginia wife, first came to Nebraska in April, 1883, she was a pretty nine-year-old with reddish-brown curls, fine skin and dark blue eyes. Her positive personality was apparent even at this age, and friends remember the little girl dressed in a leopard-skin fabric coat and hat, sitting on the base shelf in Miner Brothers' General Store in the town of Red Cloud to have a pair of shoes fitted, and discoursing, with some prompting from her father, on Shakespeare, English history, and life in Virginia.

Charles Cather had been toying with the idea of coming West ever since Willa, his first child, was born in 1873. Tuberculosis in the family, the damp climate of Winchester, Virginia, and stories about the new country from earlier homesteaders, including his father,

mother and brother George, whetted his interest still
more, and when in 1883 his four-storied sheep barn
burned, he and Willa's mother packed up their belong-
ings in Confederate paper currency and took the first
train they could get to Red Cloud. The journey, complete with the red-plush seats of the Burlington & Missouri coaches, must have been similar to Willa's descrip-
tion, 35 years later, of young "Jim Burden's" trip from
Virginia to "Black Hawk" (Red Cloud) in the opening
pages of the autobiographical *My Ántonia*.

And as "Jim Burden" did, Willa and her family drove
overland 16 miles to the precinct of Catherton, where
the rest of the Cather family had homesteaded a decade
before. Willa's first playmates were the neighbor children, the Lambrechts, whose parents had come from
Germany. "Leedy" Lambrecht (the name is now dis-
tortedly pronounced Lambert) was the same age as
Willa, and played with her in the attic of Grandfather
Cather's big frame house where the Charles Cather
family had moved. They dressed in adult's garments,
pretending to be clowns, or went snake-hunting, as "Ántonia" and "Jim" did, in the tall grass with Leedy's
brother Henry, who peeled sugar cane for them in place
of candy. But unlike "Jim," Henry was bitten by a
rattlesnake, and after his parents had given him whiskey
(everyone kept it for stomach trouble) and had tied a
piece of raw chicken meat over the bite, they took him

to Red Cloud where Dr. Damerell put ammonia into the wound. Henry didn't mind the bite so much as he did the day-long, bumpy wagon ride, with the road lurching over ridges and through buffalo-wallows to enter Red Cloud from the northwest.

*　　*　　*

The first Cather to come to America from Ireland was Jasper, a red-haired schoolteacher who taught in Western Pennsylvania before the French and Indian wars. There he married and possibly had children—the record is not complete—but in any case when the fort near where he lived was burned by the French, he and other settlers fled, returning later to find their lands occupied by others. Sometime during this trouble his wife died and he married her sister who bore him several children and died. To his third marriage, with Sarah Moore in 1786, was born James Cather, father of William Cather and the great-grandfather of Willa.

Once, after her fame had spread abroad, Willa had a letter from a distant cousin in England asking if she were a descendant of that Jasper Cather who had gone to America from Northern Ireland. During the ensuing correspondence the English cousin wrote that the original family home was the Cadder Idris, a mountain in Wales whose name means "Giant Chair," that an ancestor had fought for Charles I and that in appreciation Charles II had later given land in Ireland to the Cather twins, Edmund and Bertram. (Willa had twin aunts, twin cousins, and twin nieces.)

It is possible that some of the family went into Scotland, as the book "The Surnames of Scotland" by George F. Black, PhD. (1946) lists the name "Catter" or "Cather" in the parish of Kilmaronock, Dumbartonshire, and states that the old Earls of Lennox had at one time their residence at Catter.

Jasper Cather, in partnership with Hamilton Cooper, also of Ireland, cleared and settled land in Virginia. After a time Jasper bought his partner's share and the latter returned to Ireland without giving his friend a clear title. In July 1812 Jasper died leaving the property on Flint Ridge to his sons, James and David, who soon after petitioned the General Assembly of Virginia that the title be cleared. They cited the following facts: that their father had fought in the Revolution, that he had duly purchased the land from Cooper, that the latter had returned to Ireland which residence, in view of the present war (1812), made him an enemy alien and therefore his property titles belonged to the state. Their request was granted. James Cather became a leader in forest conservation in Virginia. (Many years later, in honor of his great-granddaughter Willa, also a tree-lover, the women's clubs of Nebraska planted five

[4]

acres of trees in Halsey Forest near Broken Bow, Nebraska.)

Flint Ridge lay about a mile east of that part of Jeremiah Smith's land grants which later William Cather, Willa's grandfather, purchased. On this site he erected a large brick residence and named it Willow Shade Farm. Jeremiah Smith, grandfather of Emily Ann Caroline Smith, wife of William Cather and grandmother of Willa, received grants of land from Lord Fairfax, Baron of Cameron, dated September 30, 1762. Miss Cather referred to Lord Fairfax and his retinue in the somewhat Poe-esque story, "A Night at Greenway Court," published first in the "Nebraska Literary Magazine," 1896, and later, April 2, 1900, in "The Library" at Pittsburgh.

In 1777 Harrison Taylor bought from the Smiths a strip of land on Back Creek and built "The Big Mill," a flour mill on the Great Road leading from Winchester to Romney. When the North Western Turnpike was constructed, engineers changed the location of the road at the creek crossing and left the mill to the south. This mill may have been the Seibert Mill or the Seiberts (sometimes spelled Sibert) may have had a saw mill or both mills. In any case, members of the Cather family who went from Nebraska to visit in Virginia, feel that "The Big Mill" is the mill of *Sapphira and the Slave Girl,* Willa's novel of pre-war Virginia.

[5]

Rachael E. Boak, Willa's maternal grandmother, was a Seibert, and evidence points to her as the prototype of "Rachael," the novel's heroine. Family records show that the Seibert Mill after 1856 was operated by Henry Seibert, brother to Mrs. Boak, who, as the novel indeed suggests, had married a wealthy woman and had kept a number of slaves. The Cathers themselves, although they hired negro help, were not slave owners.

William L. Boak of Berkeley County, Willa's maternal grandfather, served in the House of Delegates of Virginia from 1845 to 1846, at the same time that James Cather, Willa's great-grandfather, represented Frederick County. Mr. Boak died when his children were quite young. Family friends think that Mrs. Boak for a time ran an exclusive boarding house in Richmond or Washington, D.C. On her return she lived about a mile and a half west from the Cather family, beyond the town of Back Creek Valley, and many years later migrated to Red Cloud with the Charles Cathers.

Out of this pre-war Virginia period of the family history Willa wove, about 80 years later, the story of "Sapphira." In doing so, she found it difficult to reconstruct herself at the age of five, when she had first heard the stories, and in the latter part of the book she actually allowed this five-year-old to appear, an intrusion she declared to be a serious literary fault.

The Family

Of these memories Stephen Vincent and Rosemary Benét wrote:

All experience has been grist to Miss Cather's slow, fine-grinding mill. . . . *Sapphira and the Slave Girl* goes back to her earliest days in Winchester. It is as though she had looked back affectionately at her childhood and thought, 'Why, there is something I have never used!' and recalled it with the clearness of morning air. So clear was this part of her life that the speech of the people, white and black, as she had heard it as a child, came back to her as if it had been stored on phonograph records in her brain.

When as a young woman Willa visited an aunt in Winchester, she felt, wrote the Benéts, that as she went down a road she knew what was coming next all the way along. *Sapphira* started as a complete history of the manners and customs of the Shenandoah Valley, and wound up with Willa cutting out all background that was not essential to her story. "I weighed what I cut out—and it came to a good six pounds."

The Civil War found William Cather living at Willow Shade Farm in a beautiful brick residence heated by a fireplace in each room. The home was surrounded by great willows; a stream ran through the front yard and a spring from the mountain supplied the spring house with continuous cool, running water.

William Cather was a Unionist, a fact which hurt his Southern father, brothers and sisters. His sons, George and Charles (Willa's father) were too young for conscription at the opening of the war, but as the years passed, they went over into West Virginia which had become a state in 1863 and early broke away from Confederate control. James Cather, William's father and a member of the Virginia Secession Committee, actually opposed both secession and slavery, but he believed in states' rights and his sympathies always remained with the South.

Mrs. Boak, Willa's maternal grandmother, had three sons in the Confederate Army. Willa, named Willa Love Cather in honor of Dr. Love, the family doctor in Virginia, later took the name Willa Sibert Cather in honor of her uncle Willie Sibert Boak, who died at 19, a soldier of the Thirty-third Virginia Regiment. It was to his memory that she promised, in her poem "The Namesake," *April Twilights*, 1903, that she alone would achieve enough fame for "two who bore the name."

The war years were particularly difficult for those who lived practically between the battle fronts, yet the friendships of the Valley were not destroyed. Once during a raid a neighbor warned the Cathers, "The Confederates are going to raid soon and take all the stock of Northern sympathizers. Bring your animals over to

my barn and they'll be safe." William accepted the offer and soon, when Union scouts threatened, he had an
opportunity to return the favor.

After the war William Cather was appointed deputy
sheriff of Frederick County and his two sons served
with him. As a Unionist he was the only man in the
community left with enough money to hire a Baptist
minister to conduct a school at Willow Shade. All the
children—Southern sympathizers included—were invited to attend. He sent some of the older children,
including his son Charles and Virginia Boak, to school
in Baltimore. Charles and Virginia were married at
Widow Boak's home in December, 1872, and according to a letter from Charles to his brother George in
Nebraska, Willa was born on December 7, 1873. Considerable conjecture has arisen on this point: the University of Nebraska records give her birth date as 1874,
while the epitaph on her tomb in East Jaffrey, New
Hampshire, gives the date as 1876.

William Cather and his wife Caroline first visited
Nebraska in 1874 to spend the winter with their son
George. Several of William's brothers had died of tuberculosis, his daughters were ill with it, and one of the
twins, Retta, had died that fall. William himself was
not well, and he found the dry climate of Nebraska
helped him. In the spring of '75, he and his wife returned to Virginia with the plan to move West, but

the death of his father complicated business affairs and it was not until 1877 that they were able to do so. The delay may have shortened William's life and that of his ailing daughter, Jennie Cather Ayres, who was by 1877 a widow with a baby. The house at Willow Shade was damp from the humid climate of the Valley and from the fact that the spring supplying water to the house from the mountain ran directly into one of the rooms. By the time the family started for Nebraska, Jennie was so ill that there was some doubt. as to whether she could make the trip. Her parents put her on a stretcher, and although she survived the journey, she died two weeks later and was buried in an orchard of young apple trees on her brother's farm. In "Macon Prairie," a poem from her *April Twilights,* Willa Cather eulogized her aunt's pioneer spirit—a spirit stronger than death, and one which foresaw the opening up of the new prairie land.

After Jennie's death, there remained to William Cather only one daughter, Alverna, a widow with a son, Kyd Clutter. She married again, had a daughter, Wilella Paine, but when the baby was only 18 months old, Alverna died in a spell of severe coughing. William and Caroline Cather, then, had three orphaned grandchildren. There was ample suggestion in the facts for Willa's choice of her own pioneer grandparents for the

The Family

"Grandfather and Grandmother Burden" in *My Ántonia*.

Grandfather Cather was a devout Baptist who spent hours reading the Bible to his sometimes unwilling grandchildren and intoning beautifully-worded but interminable prayers. It was no accident that "Grandfather Burden" in *My Ántonia* said a Protestant prayer over the suicide-grave of "Papa Shimerda," the homesick Bohemian—Grandfather Cather indeed said a prayer over the grave of the real-life "Shimerda," unshriven and buried in unhallowed ground at a crossroads (he now lies in the Bohemian cemetery near Bladen, Nebraska). Earnest but domineering, he maintained the patriarchal ideal of family life. He had not allowed Charles to play his violin on Sunday and he forbade cards. But whenever anyone even hinted a criticism of him, Willa's mother would exclaim, "Many's the time I'd have gone barefoot and hungry if it hadn't been for Grandfather Cather." She was thinking of the difficult days after the war.

After the death of her last daughter, Grandmother Cather always wore mourning. Wherever she went, her face was shrouded in a veil of black silk with a wide border which was fastened to the tight fitting bonnet of that day. Devout, but in a less violent way than her husband, Caroline Cather was mild and gentle. She was a great favorite with Willa and it was she who gave Willa money with which to complete her University education.

II

"Manna in the Wilderness"

GEORGE CATHER and Frances A. Smith, a girl from Boston and a graduate of Mount Holyoke Female Seminary were married in June of 1873. Both were teachers. After a honeymoon in New England they entrained for Nebraska, alighting at Juniata, the railroad station nearest their homestead lands. George Cather hired a man with team and wagon, measured the circumference of one of the back wheels, tied a rag on the rim so they could more easily count the revolutions and started across the prairie. George had a compass to keep him going in the right direction. His wife sat in the back of the wagon, counted revolutions and computed mileage. (The "jolt of the tied wheel" appeared later in Willa's poem "Macon Prairie.") When they had, according to calculations, reached their homestead, they drove on a bit to what they judged to be the center of their property, just to make sure they were really on their own land—and pitched a tent for the night.

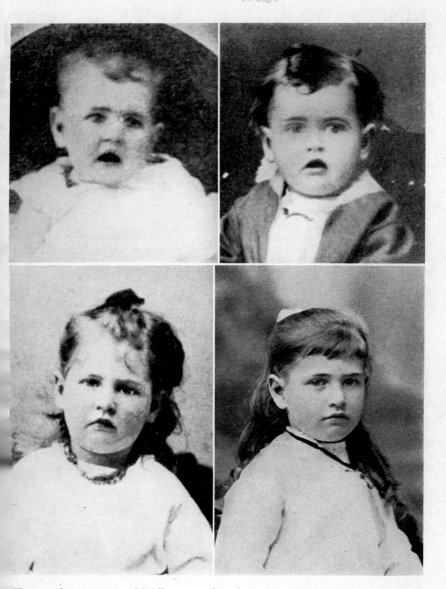

These earliest pictures of Willa were taken during her Virginia childhood, when the Cather family lived in the Shenandoah Valley and Willa heard the stories she was to remember later in *Sapphira and the Slave Girl*. In the picture at lower right she is wearing a cross made of the hair of both her father and her mother and tipped at the ends with gold.

James Cather, Willa's great-grandfather, was in the Secession Legislature. He and brother David settled at Flint Ridge, Va. George Cather (right) homesteaded in Nebraska in 1873. A little of him is in "Mr. Wheeler," in *One of Ours*.

Grandmother and Grandfather Cather were prototypes of the "Burden" grandparents in the autobiographical *My Ántonia*. William Cather, a stern religiou man, always looked older than he was because of bald head and imposing beard

The Family

Mrs. George Cather, or Aunt Frank as Willa always called her, unpacked her white sheets, white blankets and made a bed, but in the middle of their first night a prairie fire swept down on them. It had been an exceptionally dry fall and the flames traveled as fast as a galloping horse. The teamster, versed in pioneer ways, started a back fire, helped them move their equipment onto the blackened earth, and settled them down again.

When morning came, Aunt Frank looked with dismay at her blackened bed-clothes. And when she inquired about water, she found there was none closer than the Cowley's place, two miles away. George walked there with a small pail, found the Cowleys had to haul their water from wherever they could find it—sometimes from Red Cloud, sixteen miles southeast.

So scarce was water on the Divide (that broad plateau of land between the Little Blue and the Republican Rivers) that the Cathers could use it only for cooking and drinking. Sometimes it became so stale and slimy they could not bear it, and their tongues and lips were swollen and cracked; but they dared not waste a drop. Finally, George found a barrel which he could mount on a pair of runners and drag over the prairie. Although the barrel had been used previously for kerosene, both were so starved for water that they ignored the peculiar flavor.

To alleviate the terrifying loneliness of the new country, Aunt Frank organized and took active part in the Sunday School at Catherton (the name almost immediately chosen for that precinct) and in the "Literaries," or cultural programs held at different homes. Willa once said that Aunt Frank distributed more manna in the wilderness than anyone else. She led the singing and taught a class of young people, many of whom later attended high school and went on to the State University. The young people admired her intellectual attainments—in some of her presentations of Emerson and other transcendentalists they caught a glimpse of a different life. Willa, herself no mean distributor of manna, was not displeased when people told her she "took after" her Aunt Frank.

Aunt Frank read a great deal, absently twisting a front lock of hair. She had five children, two of whom were twins, Oscar and Frank. After their birth, she left Grandmother Cather in charge and visited "back East" —the trip of a frontierswoman returning briefly to "culture" which suggested to Willa the theme of the poignant "A Wagner Matinee," a short story first published in "Everybody's" and later in *Youth and the Bright Medusa*.

Her son, "G. P." Cather, killed on active service in the first World War, was plainly the inspiration for Claude in *One of Ours*, a sensitive boy who could never quite reconcile himself to the devouring materialism of his farm community, or for that matter, of early 20th Century America. After her son's death, Aunt Frank gave Willa his letters. Willa, thoroughly aroused and interested, told friends, "I never knew he was that kind of fellow. He revealed himself in his letters, and let me tell you, he's going to be my next book." When the book was finished she said, "It took more out of me than any book I ever wrote."

The hero (she told a reporter) is just a red-headed prairie boy. I always felt it was presumptuous and silly for a woman to write about a male character but by a chain of circumstances I came to know that boy better than I know myself. I have cut out all picture-making because that boy does not see pictures. It was hard to cease to do the thing that I do best, but we all have to pay a price for everything we accomplish and because I was willing to pay so much to write about this boy, I felt that I had a right to do so.

The letters that Miss Cather received from thousands of soldiers who appreciated the book meant more to her than critical acclaim. In 1925, she said in New York that of all her books she liked the one best that "all the high-brow critics knock. . . . I don't think it has as few faults perhaps as *My Ántonia* or *A Lost Lady*, but any story of youth, struggle and defeat can't be as smooth in outline and perfect in form as just a portrait. When you have an inarticulate young man butting his way through the world you can't pay that much attention to form."

Miss Cather said that Claude was the best tribute she could pay to Nebraska. It was a two-edged tribute, but *One of Ours* won the Pulitzer prize for the best novel of 1922.

Aunt Frank died in 1922 before she had an opportunity to read the book. The characters of the high-handed Nat Wheeler and his defeated wife take some of their color from Uncle George and Aunt Frank. George Cather was one of the first men in Webster County, one of its largest landholders, and a surveyor of the boundaries for the present precincts. As Willa remarked, he had come West sometime shortly after Creation. The setting of the Wheeler house in *One of Ours* is that of the 30-room George Cather home, still standing in Catherton, "the tall house with its lighted windows" that clutches at the heart.

III

"Think Not I Forget"

WHEN WILLA WAS BORN in December of 1873, her mother and father were living with Grandmother Boak, and Willa was named for her two grandfathers, both Williams. When she was not quite a year old the family moved into Willow Shade, on the road to Winchester, Virginia, while Grandfather Cather and his wife made their first trip West. There in the lovely big house which had served as headquarters for Union Army officers and where Willa spent the earliest years of her childhood, Charles decided to repair family relationships severely strained by the war. His wife Virginia, a loyal Southerner, dressed in her most charming clothes, called on all Charles' relatives inviting them to a party at Willow Shade. Unwilling to disappoint the young hostess, they forgot their displeasure with her father-in-law William and his Unionist family, came to the party, and the breach was healed.

Thereafter when any argument about the war arose between Charles and Virginia, he would begin to criticize John Brown, and before she realized it, Virginia was in agreement with him, and the dispute had vanished.

Charles Cather bought sheep in the hills of Virginia, fattened them at Willow Shade and took them to market in Baltimore. He was fond both of his sheep and his shepherd dogs, for whom he made special protective shoes against the damp, rugged ground of the Shenandoah Valley. It was these days with her father that Willa remembered when she wrote "Swedish Mother,"

[17]

a poem about a little girl's love for her shepherd father.
The red-haired child in the poem to whom the tale is
told is one of Willa's nieces.

At Willow Shade was an enormous four-story barn
with a mill which ground feed for the sheep. When
that barn burned from spontaneous combustion, Charles
decided to head for Nebraska. The family arrived there
in April, 1883, and lived in Grandfather Cather's house
while the latter went back to Virginia and Grandmother
moved in with her son George. Willa, then nine and
already quite decided in her tastes, considered herself
too old to play with her little cousins Carrie and
Blanche, an immature six and four. But Roscoe, Willa's
six-year-old brother, had no such scruples, and entertained the girls with Southern legends of the long-
pawed growlies and the short-pawed growlies. He
pretended to talk with these mythical creatures under
the willows about the pond, and the little girls crawled
everywhere after him to find them. Once, when they
covered Roscoe with wheat in the bin, Blanche was sent
to tell Willa that he was dead and that she must come
to view the body; characteristically, Willa paid no attention.

Grandfather Cather's house, Willa's first home in
Webster County, had been built on two levels, with a
basement and its kitchen entered from a draw, or ra-
vine, and a first floor which opened out on the hillside.

(In *My Ántonia,* Jim Burden recalls: " 'Down in the kitchen' struck me as curious; it was always 'out in the kitchen' at home.") Once, during cold weather, Willa's mother, lying ill in the kitchen, happened to look up and see smoke curling around the chimney in the ceiling above her. She screamed for help and Margie, the mountain girl from Virginia who worked for them, came and carried her out. After that experience both Margie and she were badly shaken up—even though the fire was quickly put out by Will Andrews, Mrs. Cather's nephew, who blistered his hands furiously drawing water from the well.

Perhaps the fact that the doctor had to come fourteen miles from Red Cloud influenced Charles to move into town, and perhaps he may also have been thinking of his children's education. Breaking the prairie sod for planting and building was a whole-family affair, and the rural school, conducted for the first time in the Catherton community in 1883, had only a three-month term. In the fall of 1884 Charles Cather sold his stock and equipment and moved into Red Cloud, then a busy railroad town of 2,500, where he opened an office, made farm loans, wrote abstracts, and sold insurance. His two years' study of law in a Quaker college in Baltimore helped him in his new business.

The story-and-a-half rented frame house into which the Cathers moved in 1884 was far too cramped for the large family. They had planned to buy a larger one, but that was sold before they could make an offer, and the smaller house remained the only one available. At first the children slept downstairs but later, as the family increased, the boys slept in the attic (as indeed the Kronborg children did in *Song of the Lark*. The excitement of sleeping in the attic must have made a deep impression on Willa, who as late as 1945 wrote about it with great feeling in her last story "The Best Years.") Margie had her room in a loft over the kitchen while Bess, Willa's cousin, stayed downstairs with the small children and later had the front end of the upstairs curtained off.

Sentimental enough about it in later years, Willa undoubtedly resented the crowded little house built by a Red Cloud lumberman who, Willa complained, had used leftovers and odd pieces. Curiously enough, the house had a duplicate on the other side of town, and must therefore have been made from some kind of plan, but Willa couldn't help but remember the great, classic house in Virginia, with its servants and fireplaces. As times grew harder, Mr. Cather claimed it was better business for him to pay rent and loan money than to buy or build. Consequently, the family stayed on in the house with its queer, 14-foot ceilings and attic heated only by the brick chimney. The children undressed downstairs, put on heavy slippers and robes, took hot bricks wrapped in wool to bed with them, and slept under plenty of quilts and blankets. In time, Willa had her own room finished under the eaves in the north wing. It was papered with a large rose pattern, and was called by the children "The Rose Bower." Bess papered her end of the large attic room with a pumpkin design and called it "The Pumpkin Bower."

Willa's Grandmother Boak lived with the Cathers until her death in 1893. Although she had suffered a broken hip while struggling to shut the Cathers' big backyard gate in a Nebraska windstorm, and consequently had great difficulty in getting about, she was always active about the house. Rising at dawn, she dressed in a full-skirted print dress, soft collar rolled at the throat, buttons down the waist front. Her dark hair barely touched with gray was parted in the middle and drawn back into a low knot. Mornings, she wore a colored apron and worked in the kitchen, where, lacking the modern conveniences of all kitchens at the time, she found more than enough to do. In addition to the nine members of the family, there were two extra paying guests for the noon meal. Like most middle-western towns of the '80's, Red Cloud had no eating places except the hotels, which refused to serve meals to any but registered guests, and the railroad restaurant which could have accommodated them but was about a mile from the center of town. As a result, some of the young men, friends of Willa's cousin Bess, found it convenient to take their noon meal at the Cathers', where the food was excellent. Grandmother Boak was an expert cook.

Willa's devotion to her grandmother found voice in the poem, "Grandmither, Think Not I Forget," in *April Twilights*. And there is more than a suggestion of Grandmother Boak and her loyal friend Margie in "Old Mrs. Harris," just as there is something of Willa's parents in the Mr. and Mrs. Templeton of that story—a bitter account of the indifference of young people to the very old in which Willa, clearly "Vicky" in the story, indicts herself perhaps more scathingly than she does anyone else.

But before considering any of Miss Cather's characters as real portraits, one must remember what she said of all her fictional people:

They are all composites of three or four persons. I do not quite understand it, but certain persons seem to coalesce naturally when one is working up a story. I believe most authors shrink from actual portrait painting. It seems so cold blooded, so heartless, so indecent almost, to present an actual person in that intimate fashion, stripping his very soul.

Willa loved her father, a Southern gentleman refined almost to the point of delicacy. He was quite unlike his aggressive older brother George, who was

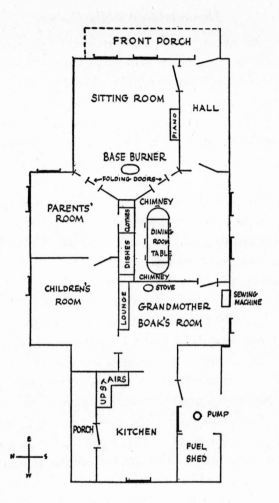

Downstairs plan of Willa's girlhood home. Her room was upstairs in the north wing, and it was always kept locked when
she was away.

intent on making money and participating in public affairs. In fact, the one time Charles Cather found himself in the limelight, he did not like it at all. Neither did Willa. . . .

The town feud started quietly enough when Mr. Cather was put on a committee to investigate whether or not the county treasurer had been accepting interest on county funds for his own use; but the tension soon flamed into open hostility between those known as the "Big Eight" and the friends of the exploiters of the county treasury, which at that time handled a considerable amount of money.

Among the "Big Eight" were Willa's father, Dr. G. E. McKeeby, a local political figure as well as the Cather family physician, Mr. Miner from the general store, Mr. Wiener, a Red Cloud German-Jewish merchant and friend of the Cathers, and ex-Governor Silas Garber. (It is interesting to note that every one of these gentlemen appeared later as important characters in Willa Cather stories.) They tried at first to fight their battle through one of the local papers, but when this didn't work, Mr. Cather started editing a paper on their behalf. He liked neither the publicity nor the conflict, however, and the "Big Eight" soon imported a newspaper man named Metzger from Omaha to handle their publicity. During the political confusion of this period (1887 to 1890) Red Cloud had five newspapers.

Willa took an avid interest in the whole affair and helped where she could.

The opposition kept up a running fire of accusations against Dr. McKeeby, then Mayor, and Mr. Cather, an alderman. When Willa's father visited the Hastings jails to get data prior to building a jail in Red Cloud, the press accused him of seeking bonuses and protecting his friend, "Uriah Heep McKeeby." An old story about Dr. McKeeby's having given medical attention to one of Red Cloud's "ladies of the evening" when she broke her leg was revived and reworked deftly to imply that the relationship had not been exactly that of doctor and patient. The good doctor was also accused of refusing to see a dying child. The Red Cloud "Chief" of Nov. 1, 1889, had things like this to say:

Dock McKeeby and Charley Cather who have taken more bonus notes and more usury off the poor people of this county than any other set of men are now posing as the farmers' friends.

We must have stirred the Jersey Lilly and his helper, Cholles Cather up in great shape . . . McKeeby don't like to be told of his outrageous bonuses in Webster County and it makes Cholles Cather's hide turn blue with rage to be exposed.

The "Cholles" was a jibe at Virginia accents. The "Chief" went on to say that Dr. McKeeby had failed in medicine and therefore had gone into politics (he was, in fact, a lawyer as well as a doctor) and that both he and Mr. Cather were liars and corrupters of government. In spite of it all, Dr. McKeeby was elected to the state senate and went to Lincoln in 1893, where he frequently saw Willa, and where he published in the University paper an appeal for better-lighted classrooms and more up-to-date facilities for the young and expanding institution. (John J. "Black Jack" Pershing was teaching military science there at the time.)

During the feud, Willa spent a great deal of time hanging about her father's office. She was unusually devoted to him and gloried in the fact that her own fine skin and dark blue eyes were like his. With gentle formality, he called her "Daughter," as he did all his girls, and even after she became famous he could not believe she had grown up. And, in spite of the critical acclaim of *O Pioneers* and *My Ántonia*, he still had difficulty in recognizing what a celebrity his daughter had become. It took Sinclair Lewis, lecturing in Omaha in 1920 to convince him: "Miss Cather is Nebraska's foremost citizen. The United States knows Nebraska because of Willa Cather's books."

At that time, the surprised Mr. Cather wrote Willa a loving letter in which he paid tribute to her genius and her success. Her reaction to the letter was to observe, somewhat superfluously, that "Father is a very modest man and he wants me to be modest."

Willa depended on her father for business advice and, still more, for companionship. During one summer that she spent at home he and two childhood friends, Carrie Miner Sherwood and Mary Miner Creighton, took Willa for a picnic on Lovely Creek, a stream in adjacent Franklin County. By the time they had started home, dusk was falling and the hills and ungraded roads north of Red Cloud made driving difficult. Mr. Cather was at the wheel and Mary was sitting beside him. He insisted that Mary sit closer to him, and when she moved over confided that he couldn't see very well in the twilight, didn't, in fact, know part of the time whether the car was going up hill or down. He wanted Mary to serve as eyes for him, but most of all he didn't want Willa to know that driving in the dark bothered him. Had she known it, she would have gotten right out and walked home. She had no confidence in cars nor in her father's driving them. He was an expert with a team, and Willa preferred horses any time.

The 1923 reprint of her book of poems *April Twilights* was a Valentine for him. After his death in 1927, she sent a copy to a friend with these words:

To remind her of my one winter in Red Cloud, after so many years, and of my gentle father to whom this book is dedicated.

That last winter in Red Cloud, spent with family and friends, followed the publication of *Death Comes for the Archbishop*. In New York, where she had been living for a number of years, Willa had had a secretary who sorted mail and answered most of it with prepared form letters; but back in Nebraska there was no one to do that and her father tried to help by reading the mail. Over some of it he would get excited and say, "Now daughter, these letters should be answered right away with personal replies."

"But father," Willa would protest, "I have a standard to maintain and I can't just dash off answers. I wouldn't get anything else done." Then she offered him and Carrie Miner Sherwood the task of sorting all her mail and picking out which correspondence should be answered with form letters. Their first morning they read forty letters and decided they hadn't known what a job they were getting into. Mr. Cather, giving it up, thought it a great joke on himself.

The death of her father was a blow that Willa could scarcely accept. She paced frantically back and forth between the house and the little Episcopal church where his body lay, wringing her hands, apparently unable to conquer the grief and panic which overwhelmed her. Acquaintances felt that her grief was not unmixed with still another emotion—fury—and a resentment that time, her greatest enemy, could effect

[28]

such changes. She knew that her home would never be the same again. Her close friends, trying to help her regain some of her lost control, talked with her for hours to convince her if they could that the beauty and fullness of his eighty years was all that one could expect from a well-spent life. At length she calmed down, but the episode serves well to illustrate her flat refusal to accept the dictatorship of time. A further demonstration of this attitude can be seen in her progressive pulling-forward of the date of her birth, which finally shows up, in the inscription on her tomb, dated three years late (1876—instead of 1873).

Willa found her mother of a far different temperament from her gentle father. Always meticulous in appearance, never stepping out of her bedroom without first being perfectly groomed, Virginia Boak Cather allowed no one to see her until her lovely hair had been pinned up. Willa, even as a child, sensed that some of the neighbors thought her mother haughty, and perhaps Willa as an adult took on some of the characteristics that casual acquaintances had found a little upsetting in her mother. She was well aware that her mother was behaving in the Southern genteel tradition, and throughout her life shared something of her mother's benevolent, if distant, desire to champion the underprivileged or the misunderstood.

Mrs. Cather was not one to be "put upon." Apparently a much more positive and strong-willed person than her husband (although in actuality she dutifully accepted without question his occasional family decisions) she ordered the household, her steel-gray eyes unwavering as she disciplined, severely when necessary. She had an immense store of energy and was fiercely devoted to what she considered the proper way of doing things. It was she, like "Thea's" mother in *Song of the Lark,* who recognized that her oldest daughter was unusually eager to learn; and although Mr. Cather thought Willa might teach for a couple of years after her high school graduation, Mrs. Cather could see immediately that the girl should go on to college at once.

Sometimes in later years the mother was to sigh in exasperation over this famous daughter. For one thing, Willa, when she came home, wanted no parties given for her, although she always welcomed the family gatherings and the one inevitable dinner for the "old ladies" whom she had known when she was a child. For another, Mrs. Cather, who prided herself on her knowledge of high fashion, frequently objected to Willa's way of dressing and particularly her violent color combinations. Willa admitted that she loved colors like a savage, but her rebellion against fashion was perhaps as much a revolt against maternal interference as it was an intense dislike of the corseted discomfort of "civilized" apparel.

Willa did as she pleased, even when both her parents objected strongly, as they did the summer she put up an ugly canvas roof and sides on the upper front porch of their Red Cloud home. She liked to be outdoors but she didn't want anyone gazing at her. What her temporary canvas structure did to the appearance of the house was of no importance to her.

Although she would not follow Mrs. Cather's advice as to clothes and social functions, Willa nevertheless knew how to please her mother and with what gifts to do it: jewelry, lovely lingerie, imported perfumes. All the Cather children enjoyed buying their mother extravagant personal things. They were proud of her regal bearing, and they knew she would show them off to better advantage than anyone they knew. Although she had borne seven children, she carried herself erect, with dignity. A handsome woman, she maintained the strictest standards of poise, carried a small parasol to match her costume, and whenever possible, wore fresh violets. There was a conflict between Willa and her mother, but always proud of her daughter, Mrs. Cather's favorite gift to friends, in later years, was an autographed copy of one of Willa's books.

The seven Cather children, the last three born in Red Cloud, were: Willa, Roscoe, Douglas, Jessica, Jim,

Elsie and Jack. As the oldest child, Willa began by leading her brothers; but by the time she had come back
from a year at the University, she discovered that the
three-year gap in age between herself and Roscoe wasn't
too great for companionship.

The summer Willa was 20, she and Roscoe spent
some time in Catherton with their Uncle George. The
"New Virginia" settlement near Catherton, comprised
of farming families who had come out from Winchester,
held periodical "literaries." At the one Willa and Roscoe attended, Willa listened to a discussion of Emerson,
and concluded, in a letter to her college friends in Lincoln, that the farmers understood transcendentalism as
well as or better than most university students. The
other part of the evening's program was a series of vocal
selections by the daughter of the family in whose house
the "literary" was being held. She sang in a grating
voice, this unhappy soul, twelve selections with encores,
and when with her last number she began, "Pray does
this music charm thy heart?" Willa was ready to ex-
plode. The proud mother of the vocalist bought fifty
copies of the paper carrying an account of the affair
and sent them to friends in the East. And a similarly
proud mother's exploitation of her daughter's mediocre
singing talents found its way, 27 years later, into the
performance of Lily Fisher in Willa's *Song of the Lark*.
She forgot nothing.

The Family

During the same summer Willa and Roscoe climbed Uncle George's fifty-foot windmill tower to see the moon rise. The two got so interested in watching a storm come up, with the red harvest moon in the East, the clouds and lightning in the West, and the cattle huddling in the corrals below, that they forgot their own precarious position. When the wind struck, they were still fifty feet in the air. Willa had to take off her outer skirts to get down, and in spite of Roscoe's help she blistered her hands clinging to the narrow ladder. The experience was not without profit to Willa, however, who seven years later built around it her first big magazine story, "Eric Hermannson's Soul" ("Cosmopolitan," 1900) hailed by at least one European critic as a "psychological masterpiece."

In Red Cloud Willa liked to buy treats for her younger brothers and sisters. And when her friends visited in the crowded Red Cloud home they were surrounded by the children, a fact both worrying and amusing to Willa, who once bribed Jim with two nickels and a bottle of pop to go into the country with his father. However, she didn't specify how long he was to stay, and escaping his father's eye, he caught a ride back with a farmer, and appeared in time to greet Willa's guest with affectionate little-boy advances, if not outright blackmail for some "special new kind of candy" he'd heard they had down at the store.

On another occasion, Willa's guest was to be a girl with a slight speech defect, and Willa explained to Jim that he must not make any comments about the affliction. All went well for a day-and-a-half. Then to her horror, Willa overheard Jim in the next room: "You know, I like you and I can understand you just fine. You're not at all like Willie said. Why, she said I couldn't understand a word you'd say, that you just went wangh! wangh! wangh! all the time."

Willa liked to tell a story of three-year-old sister Elsie. One season had been dry and everyone was hoping for rain. When Elsie asked her mother what made the rain, her mother said that God did. The next day for the first time that season, a neighbor in desperation turned on his two lawn sprinklers. Elsie came running in calling for "Willie" and explaining that there were *two* little gods out in the neighbor's yard, just raining like everything.

Willa entered the University of Nebraska in the fall of 1890 and graduated in 1895, but for most of her vacations she returned to Red Cloud. Whenever she got home the children would be dressed in their best to welcome her, and at each homecoming, she wrote back to friends in Lincoln, found them more beautiful and cleverer than she had remembered.

In the late fall of '95 Willa went home to stay. As it is for many a new graduate, it was the most discourag-

ing period of her life. Isolated from her family, too depressed with her "ignorance" and "lack of progress" to
work on any manuscripts, Willa felt the additional burden of her family's great expectations of her. Unwilling,
like the "Lucy Gayheart" and "Thea Kronborg" of her
novels, to support herself through any commonplace occupation, and unable to get on with what she really
wanted to do, Willa put in a frustrated six months until,
to the relief of everyone, she took a proffered job as editor of the "Home Monthly" in Pittsburgh, Pa.

To help her pass the time during her "exile" she occasionally accompanied her brother to parties. One was a
New Year's Dance, and in her bad humor she found the
affair quite "rowdy." Since several girls had expected
Douglas to invite them, he put on a special show by taking Willa instead, ordering flowers from Lincoln and
deporting himself as a great gentleman. The dance was
held in a large hall, the floor of which was covered with
wax shavings so rough they made dancing almost impossible. The seats were crude planks laid across chairs; the
boys and girls used the same dressing room. But what
shocked the already worldly Willa most was the serving
of sandwiches in a bushel basket. Altogether, with her
genteel University tastes, she felt she might be as far
from civilization as Siberia.

In February of 1896 she engineered a wedding break-
fast for her cousin Retta Ayres who married Hugh

Miner. She imported strawberries, fresh tomatoes and water cress from Chicago and felt herself getting quite domestic. Not long after, her parents left her in charge while they went to Hastings. During their absence brother Jack, aged four, swallowed two pennies and Jim cut his lip. The weather was so cold that Willa did not ride her bicycle, but left it for Jessica who didn't seem to mind the weather. Willa despairingly reported to friends that she was acting as a hospital matron, and that she was so tired of reading "Alice in Wonderland," which she had already read Jim sixteen times, that she had switched to "The Arabian Nights."

When Roscoe was home, he and Willa collected botanical specimens and mounted them. Willa was interested in plants; but after Roscoe had gone away to teach, Willa came to appreciate Douglas and to enjoy going to dances with him. Later, when Douglas worked for the railroad in Cheyenne, Wyoming, as station agent, Willa visited him and went on a real pioneer camping trip to Laramie.

"The Affair At Grover Station," a railroad murder mystery published in "The Library," Pittsburgh, 1900, was written with his assistance. He also checked the technical details in the wreck scene of *Song of the Lark*, and during his years with the railroad, he published some stories of his own in the railroad papers.

Willa's first acquaintance with the Southwest began

when Douglas was working for the Southern Pacific and invited her to visit him, enticing her with tales of his fine living arrangements. He and a brakeman named Tooker (the brakeman of *Song of the Lark*) had a little house and an old Englishman, whom Douglas had found drunk under a watering tank, for a cook. When Henry the cook learned that Douglas's sister was really coming, he was so moved that his ensuing celebration kept him out of commission until Willa had already been there two days.

Willa was delighted with Henry's French and his knowledge of continental ways, and Henry turns up, almost verbatim, as one of the liveliest characters of *The Professor's House*. Douglas took her all over the countryside—the mesas, the pueblos, the painted desert, and the Southwest may well have been the place for the maturing of Willa's talent as much as that of "Thea" in *Song of the Lark*. Much of Willa's holiday can be found in *The Professor's House*, but the volume which deals most fully with this part of the United States is *Death Comes for the Archbishop*.

Douglas finally went to California where he prospered in the oil business. He never married. Roscoe, after attending the University of Nebraska, returned to teaching. He married, had three daughters (a pair of them twins) and composed fairy tales to entertain them. For a while he wrote abstracts, then joined Doug-

las in Wyoming, and helped found the town of Grey-
bull. For the last forty years of his life Roscoe was a
banker. Both brothers preceded Willa in death.

The four younger Cather children are living. Jessica
married and had three children: one a physician, one a
business man, one the wife of a physician. James has
a daughter and a son, Charles, the only boy to carry on
the family name. Elsie, of Lincoln, Nebraska, formerly
a teacher in the public schools there, is now retired.
Jack has two daughters.

Willa wrote a story about Jack, or "Jack-a-boy" as
they used to call him, published in "The Saturday Evening Post," March 30, 1901. In it she described her
admiration for her little brother. She told friends that
she would give anything just to look into his eyes for
ten minutes.

The affection which she felt for her brothers and sisters extended to her nephews and nieces, and in her
will, she left them the greater part of her wealth.

The Christmas of 1927 Willa was home in Red
Cloud, and as she was arranging the crêche, her little
nephew Charles came with a toy cow which he wanted
to contribute. Willa hesitated, not wishing to deprive
him of his treasure, but he insisted on giving it to "the
Little Jesus." After *Shadows on the Rock* was published, Miss Cather wrote a friend asking if she recognized the beaver incident, a scene where the Quebec

prostitute's little boy Jacques gives away his only pos-
session, a carved wooden beaver, to "the Crêche, the
little Jesus." The friend said that she didn't. Then Miss
Cather told the story of the cow and added that since
that time, she had especially loved little Charles.

CHILDHOOD

I

"A Hundred Years of Unlived Life"

WHEN THE CATHERS moved to Red Cloud in the fall of 1884, Willa's first playmate was Mary Miner, the merchant's second daughter, who came over to welcome her with a bottle of perfume in a red plush slipper. From then on the Miner and Cather children played together continuously, and the friendship has continued to this day. Willa had been ill, with what may have been infantile paralysis, before the family moved from the country, and she was supposed to use a crutch, but she soon threw it away and learned to walk as well as anyone. In adult life walking was one of her favorite pastimes.

The children liked the warm, summer days when they could wander over the fields picking flowers and tearing off petals to see the "cheeses" inside. The Miners' barn was a delightfully large building where the children had circuses. Once a cow disappeared and they found her in the haymow. She had somehow mounted the broad stairway. It was an all-day job getting her down, and in the end she was forced to jump from the hayloft door onto a pile of hay hastily assembled in the barnyard.

The buggy-step (where the adults climbed in and out of their various conveyances) was also a favorite place, particularly on one Fourth of July when Mr. Van Brocklin, general salesman from Marshall Field's in Chicago came out with a huge box of fireworks. The children could scarcely wait for evening when the men would take out skyrockets, Roman candles, pin-wheels and other pieces. Some were fastened to the telephone pole (a private line—Red Cloud had no public telephones then) and some nailed to the buggy step. Each child had some colorful piece he could hold while it belched forth balls of color.

One skyrocket was enormous and everyone was afraid of it, yet no one wanted it rejected. The men had never heard of a launching trough, and after some discussion the intrepid Mr. Miner said he would sit in the front doorway and rest the rocket on the floor between his legs. At that time there was no porch on the house, and the children could easily observe everything from the yard. But they were afraid they might miss something, and congregated in the hall behind their father. When he touched off the fuse, the rocket shot a series of sparks which covered him thoroughly and which scattered frightened children everywhere.

Another treat was the visit of Findley Hypes, also a Marshall Field man and a wonderful singer who had even once considered opera as a career preferable to "drumming." Sadie Becker, his favorite accompanist, had come with her parents a short time previously from New York. Sadie, a vivacious and talented girl, was sixteen when she fell in love with a nineteen-year-old Red Cloud boy. Her father, when he heard they had won a dancing contest at the skating rink, threw the culprit out of the house and forbade Sadie to see him again. Somewhat disillusioned, the boy married someone else and devoted his life to making money. Sadie went away to study music and did not return to Red Cloud. The old-timers who remember Sadie's pert manner, fleet walk and charming smile feel maybe Willa was thinking of her and her affair when she wrote *Lucy Gayheart*.

Willa often went with the Miners on picnics to their ranch, southwest of town. There they could examine the well-built sod house with wooden floor, plastered walls and shingled roof; or they could race over the hills along the river and hunt Indian arrowheads. On the river's bank stood the mill which ground flour and in 1887 furnished electricity for the town. Later, the mill, probably "Jason Royce's" in *One of Ours*, burned down and Red Cloud was without electricity until the early 1900's. In the river, near the mouth of Indian Creek, stood the island where the children fished, ran barefoot on the white sandbars and hunted treasure, even as the children do in similar surroundings in Willa's early stories "The Treasure of Far Island" and "The Enchanted Bluff." Hughie Miner, the "Charlie Harling" of *My Ántonia* and one of the little boys in *A Lost Lady*, enjoyed fishing, and he used to fill his pockets with grasshoppers, now and then leaving them there. When his mother smelled something decaying she knew where to look.

The Miner children had a pony, Billy, who could be trusted to start for home either at the first drop of rain or when he began to tire. The children particularly liked to drive him to the depot. Red Cloud was on the main line of the Burlington & Missouri between Kansas City and Denver, and eight passenger trains, four eastbound and four west, passed through daily. Billy's former owner had been a trainman and the pony knew all about engines. To prove his bravery the trainmen would put a pail of water between two live engines and Billy would walk between to drink, much to the delight of those station idlers and passengers who had stopped at the station eating house. In those days there were no diners on this route west of the Missouri and before a train arrived for a meal, the train crew would wire ahead the number who might be expected. Often celebrities or show-people were among the crowd. If the troupe for some entertainment at the Opera House happened to arrive, the children were doubly delighted.

Only once was there an accident involving Billy and the gig. The children were showing the town to a visiting girl who, trying to show off, stood up and fell into the draw of sunflowers across from the Cather home. She was carried into the house and Dr. McKeeby was called. To their great satisfaction neither the children nor Billy received the blame for her broken arm.

A favorite hang-out for Willa and Mary Miner was the Miner Brothers' Store. When no one was looking they would slip upstairs to the candy barrel. They liked a certain kind of small cylinder with circles of different colors and flavors surrounding a white center with a colorful pattern—a green shamrock, a red flower, or a red-white-blue top hat. If the candy barrel were nearly empty, the girls would push a box up close, stand with noses over the rim, and one of them would take off shoes and stockings and climb in to find the candy. Usually they were caught and sent home.

Mary Miner appears in *My Ántonia* as "Julia," the musical one. Willa used to tiptoe into the house to hear Mary practice, and then tease her into playing more and more selections. Whenever Mary was too tired to

andfather Cather built this mansion at Willow Shade, near Winchester, Va. A
ion officers' headquarters during Civil War, Willa's mother was later hostess
re to South and North adherents among the Cathers, healing family breaches.

llow Shade feed barn was for sheep Mr. Cather fattened for market. Willa
ed to think of him as "The Good Shepherd." It was the burning of this barn
t finally influenced Charles Cather to leave Virginia for Nebraska.

Willa's father and mother were Charles and Virginia Boak Cather. On their golden wedding anniversary, Willa told of her first recollection of them. She said she remembered being tucked into a sleigh between them to visit friends. As they drove along on that beautiful winter's day she admired everything, the weather, the snow, the warm lap robes and finally

illa, wearing her hair cross tipped in gold, poses in her Hiawatha costume, mplete with bow and arrow. At the proper moment in her recitation she would op on one knee and shoot her arrow into the imaginary forest. The striped ckings were hand-knit from yarn so colored that the finished product would striped in the fashionable manner of the time.

This was a typical sod dugout of the 1880's, the Oscar Ramsey homestead sou of Bladen, Neb., and east of the George Cather place. Building material for t "soddies" was cut out of the earth on which they were to stand.

Willa describes the Miner home in Red Cloud as the "Harling House" in *Ántonia*. She used to watch the large south window (left) to see if Mr. Min shadow appeared. If he were not at home, she would go over and visit.

play any more, but too polite to say so, she would start a tiresome little ditty called "Pompinette" which Willa hated. On that signal Willa started for home.

Margie Miner, the third eldest sister, appears in *My Ántonia* as "Sally," the wild one, and like tomboy "Sally," had short hair even before Willa had her own chopped off in 1888. Irene Miner is "Nina," and like "Nina" had an unusual imagination. When anything went wrong, her eyes would fill with tears and she would go home. Willa often said that Irene's eyes could hold more tears than any others. *My Ántonia* is dedicated "to Carrie and Irene Miner, in memory of affections old and true."

Carrie, the "Frances Harling" of the book, was the eldest and worked as bookkeeper in the store. Older than her friend "Willie," she exerted an important influence on her during this period. In one of her notes of dedication Miss Cather wrote: "To Carrie Miner Sherwood, my fellow student of human stories," and in the flyleaf of *My Ántonia* she inscribed: "In memory of old friends whose portraits are sketched in this book."

Willa was incessantly asking questions of Carrie, until the exasperated Mr. Miner asked Carrie why she spent so much time with "that child." But Willa knew what she wanted then as later and kept on asking. In *My Ántonia*, she revealed that she was quite well aware of Mr. Miner's feelings toward her.

Mr. Miner put unbounded confidence in his daughter Carrie. Once a month when the special Burlington pay car arrived, in the evening after the banks had closed, the store was prepared to accommodate the railroad men. Mr. Miner would lay several thousands in bills on the cash counter in the office, place his six-shooter on top, and when he went to supper, would say, "Carrie, pay car tonight! There's the gun. I don't think you'll have to use it, but if you do, go ahead."

Not yet twenty, Carrie took charge (as "Frances Harling" did) when her father was out of town. When during one of these absences she was forced to make a quick decision her father later said, "Carrie, you're so positive! Doesn't it ever occur to you that you could be wrong?" She answered, "Yes, it does," and banged her fist on the table. "But I'd rather be wrong fifty percent of the time than not be able to have an opinion."

*   *   *

It was through her friendship with the Miner children that Willa came to know Annie. Miss Cather said in 1921:

One of the people who interested me most as a child was the Bohemian hired girl of one of our neighbors, who was so good to me. She was one of the truest artists I ever knew in the keenness and sensitiveness of her enjoyment, in her love of people and in her willingness to take pains. I did not realize all this as a child, but Annie fascinated me and I always had it in mind to write a story about her.

But from what point of view should I write it up? I might give her a lover and write from his standpoint. However, I thought my Ántonia deserved something better than the Saturday Evening Post sort of stuff in her book. Finally, I concluded that I would write from the point of a detached observer, because that was what I had always been.

Then I noticed that much of what I knew about Annie came from the talks I had with young men. She had a fascination for them, and they used to be with her whenever they could. They had to manage it on the sly, because she was only a hired girl. But they respected and admired her, and she meant a good deal to some of them. So I decided to make my observer a young man.

There was the material in that book for a lurid melodrama. But I decided that in writing it I would dwell very lightly on those things that a novelist would ordinarily emphasize, and make up my story of the little, every-day happenings and occurrences that form the greatest part of everyone's life and happiness.

Knowing Annie and her never-failing energy was an inspiration. The daughter of Bohemian immigrants, she had spent most of the time since she arrived in America (when she was 12) in breaking the reluctant prairie sod, struggling with the planting and harvesting and helping her widowed mother try to keep the family together. Desperation drove her to find employment in the Miner home as a "hired girl," and there, although she had never tried before, soon learned to cook and sew. When Mrs. Miner gave her permission to use the machine, she made all the clothes, shirts, jeans, overalls, and husking gloves for her own hardworking family. For herself she made everyday shoes with a cardboard insole, covered with oilcloth on the bottom and several thicknesses of suiting or denim on top. These she tied to her feet with black tape. Their flapping did not delay her in her breathless scurrying to do everything she could, and in her spare minutes she even found time (as the fictional "Ántonia" did) to pick out hickory nut-meats for one of Hughie's special Sunday cakes.

The children took Annie with them to the Opera House entertainments. Carrie saw to it that although Annie's family collected her wages, for she was under 18, there was enough left for shoes. Annie would work all day and dance all night if she could. She soon learned to copy any style of dress and much to the annoyance of some of the other girls, made herself duplicates of those she liked. When later Annie went west to marry a brakeman on the Burlington, she had many beautiful clothes, but her happiness was short-lived, for after a few weeks her lover deserted her and Annie returned to Webster County and her mother's dugout.

II

"One Clings to One's Friends So"

WILLA'S CHILDHOOD PLAYMATES continued to be her friends throughout her lifetime. For a time she lost track of Annie, but when she found her again, she never failed to visit her when she could. Annie had married a Bohemian boy, mothered a large family of which she was justly proud. Her daughters were beautiful, her sons the champions in the county weight-lifting and boxing contests and on the high school basketball and football teams.

Willa grown-up was particularly pleased with Annie's family. Always sensitive to any change in the weather, Miss Cather carried an assortment of scarfs, capes, and wraps, and when Annie's boys took her to the carriage at their farm gate, each one would have some garment draped over his arm, ready to help "Miss Cather" (Annie, like all her early friends, called her "Willie") into it or with a flourish lay it at her feet in the conveyance. After visiting that family Miss Cather, completely exhausted with excitement would exclaim: "The manners of Annie's sons would do credit to the family of a Grand Duke!"

Willa had a good time sitting at the long table in Annie's cheerful kitchen, enjoyed eating with the crowd of happy-faced children. Annie had a continental genius for inventing new dishes, and Willa liked Bohemian cooking—*kolache* and Annie's special banana cream pie. Outside the kitchen door was the food storage cave, characteristic of all middlewestern farm homes—the cave Miss Cather described in the closing pages of *My Ántonia.*

Annie's husband, the "Neighbor Rosicky" of *Obscure Destinies,* was as proud of his children as his wife was. Neighbors told him he should sell his cream, get more money, and buy more land, but he agreed with Annie ("That's right, mama!") that roses in the cheeks of their children were more important than land or money in the bank. How Miss Cather laughed when they told her about it, and how pleased she was to find Annie's children practicing the same philosophy years later.

At the Mary Lanning Hospital in Hastings, an attendant asked Annie's ailing husband who he was, and he replied, with the same pride, "I am the husband of My Ántonia!" He is now buried in the little Bohemian cemetery in the northern part of the county—the cemetery overlooking the cornfields and rich sloping pastures described in "Neighbor Rosicky." In the same cemetery lies the body of Annie's father ("Mr. Shimerda") brought there from its first resting place by the crossroads.

At one time, Willa sent Annie Pavelka a check for fifty dollars with instructions to buy herself a present, but taxes on the home place were due and Annie paid them, never revealing that the money had gone for necessities. Too proud to admit any need, the family never asked help; but Willa would inquire of mutual friends, "Is the oldest boy planting hybrid corn? If not, I shall see that he can afford it another year." She sent money repeatedly to provide seed wheat during the bitter drought years.

Annie is still living and many times a grandmother. Alert, active and interested in everything, she lives with one of her children and takes great delight in seeing old friends and showing them the fine needlework with which she still takes prizes at the county fairs, and inviting her guests to eat delicacies she has on hand, for she has not forgotten how to cook. Neither has she forgotten her trip in a "mover wagon" across Czechoslovakia to Prague at the age of twelve, nor her first days in America, nor the period when she worked in Red Cloud homes.

Her only complaint about those days was that in some

kitchens there wasn't enough butter, sugar, and cream to make the food taste right. "I had a hard life," she says still in a slight Czech accent, "but now I have things easy and the children are all so good to me." Enthusiastically, she points to the neatly arranged gifts in her dresser—presents from her children, the shawl sent her after Miss Cather's death. On her dresser stands a small photograph of "Willie" beside a package of letters telling how much Miss Cather enjoyed hearing from Annie and how during an illness she kept the letters close so she could read them whenever she felt lonely. On her walls Annie has some prints from Czechoslovakia, a gift to Miss Cather from Thomas Masaryk, first president of that country; and she cherishes in her china cupboard a set of Italian dishes, a gift from "Willie." No one is allowed to help her wash those dishes.

One of Annie's greatest pleasures is attending the movies with her children. Although past 80 and now quite hard of hearing, she still retains that "something which fires the imagination" like her namesake in the book. In her yard are apricot and peach trees grown from pits, cherry trees her son-in-law set out, strawberries, and a vegetable garden with beets, beans, carrots, turnips, tomatoes, cabbage, dill and parsley. By the front porch is a choice rose, gift from one of her sons; and she points with pride, her blue eyes sparkling, to a bit of red clover which is "just like that in the old country."

One of Annie's sons says of her, "She's wonderful—she was happier with a crust of bread and a new baby than someone else would be with a million dollars. I never saw her unhappy."

*　　*　　*

Willa Cather often stated that one of her deepest interests was the life of the foreign immigrant in America, and it is no secret that it was the struggle for adjustment of these people in their new country that formed the basis for all her most significant and enduring work. The trail into Red Cloud led past the sod house of just such a one of these families, the Fred Lambrechts, and since she liked to play with the children, Willa was often in Mrs. Lambrecht's kitchen, as usual asking questions. To this generous-hearted woman, Willa's friendliness and curiosity were commendable and she would stop her work to explain or she would demonstrate how foods were cooked or garments fashioned in the old country.

Her husband and his brother Henry had been cigar-makers in Germany, as were "Alexandra Bergson's" neighbors in *O Pioneers*, and Fred had served three years in the German army. In America they first took jobs in a cigar factory in Freeport, Illinois, and married sisters. At that time, the railroad was pushing the sale of new land at three-and-a-half to four dollars an acre, and it didn't take the brothers long to catch the property fever of the day. Knowing little of farming, they came west to break the buffalo grass sod with teams of oxen, put up sod houses, and struggled with the disheartening task of making a living out of the recalcitrant earth. Often they were discouraged, and no doubt longed for the life they had known. Then it was that the strength of the pioneer women showed itself in clinging to the soil for the sake of their children. The Lambrechts' problem, and in fact the problem of every immigrant family on the Divide, was the problem of the "Bergsons" in *O Pioneers*.

After the Cathers moved to town, the Lambrechts would stop in during their weekly shopping trip, and always Mrs. Lambrecht would bring something fresh from the farm. When Mrs. Cather fell ill with pneumonia, Mrs. Lambrecht took care of her. After Willa had left home, she frequently sent Mrs. Lambrecht gifts: hand-made woollen sweaters, scarfs from abroad, and other beautiful and useful things. During the depression years, Willa worried constantly about these friends, regretting that she had recently moved into a more expensive apartment in New York. It was not so much that they needed what she could give them, but rather that she derived great pleasure from any oppor-

tunity to express her love for them. Repeatedly she
wrote to Red Cloud merchants giving detailed instructions and sending money to buy coffee, dried fruits and
other delicacies to be dispatched to Mrs. Lambrecht.
Miss Cather knew what farming would be like in bad
years; and although her friends, who were in some ways
as reticent as Willa herself, would never write her of
their struggles, she was sure that sometimes there wasn't
enough cash to buy the select brand of coffee which
Mrs. Lambrecht so greatly enjoyed.

In later years after every Christmas season Miss
Cather sent Mrs. Lambrecht a box of greeting cards
which she had received from all over the world, thinking the sight of them would cheer her; for as years
passed, Mrs. Lambrecht was more and more confined
to her rocking chair and finally to her bed. When that
time came, Miss Cather sent a little lamp equipped
with a battery that could be placed by the bedside and
used for emergencies during the night. Especially precious to Mrs. Lambrecht was a German translation of
My Ántonia which after her death was given to the Red
Cloud Library.

Whenever Miss Cather returned to Red Cloud,
no matter what the weather, like "Miss Evangeline
Knightly" of "The Best Years" she went out to Catherton, preferably by horse and buggy. On one occasion
when the younger Lambrecht girls, Clara and Della,

were preparing lunch, they set on the table a dish of wild plum jam. Their mother reproved them in German, saying it wasn't good enough for their important guest, but Miss Cather, familiar with German, understood and would not allow the dish to be removed, adding that it was a favorite delicacy, reminiscent of the Damson plum-jam "cheese" she had enjoyed in England. At lunch, to the delight of the girls, she took several helpings.

In the days before modern methods of canning or the deep freeze, farm women preserved some foods by putting them down in lard. Miss Cather liked this recipe: Cooked green beans with partially fried sausage put in jars, covered with hot lard and sealed. When Willa visited them, the Lambrechts served and displayed whatever would please their guest. One time she admired a quilt embroidered with the flowers of the different states. As soon as possible thereafter, her friends made her a duplicate, which, she told them later, she used as a counterpane in her New York apartment.

Willa liked to visit with Julius, the younger son, who raised pure-bred white-faced cattle and who faced life with such imperturbability that he was a challenge to her understanding. Her curiosity piqued her into spending as much time as she could at the barn talking with him. Even in New York she kept informed of his affairs through the Red Cloud "Commercial Advertiser."

If "Jule" sold a prize bull or initiated new farming methods, she noted and commented on it in her next letter home. If one of her friends had a crop failure, she knew it and managed on some pretext to send a check disguised as a Valentine, a Christmas gift, or a birthday remembrance. Even after her death, the usual Christmas checks came to these intimate friends.

Another friend of Willa's early days was the hired girl, Margie, who appears as "Mahailey" in *One of Ours,* as "Mandy" in "Old Mrs. Marris" and as "Poor Marty" in *April Twilights.* Margie's mother had worked for Mrs. Cather in Virginia, and when the poor woman, mother of fifteen, heard that the Cathers were moving to Nebraska, she begged them to take the girl along.

As a child in Virginia Willa had gone with Margie to hunt flowers, and she realized that she had to be responsible for herself and the vague Margie also. When Willa learned to read, she tried to teach Margie, but the poor girl succeeded only in learning to tell time.

In the Cather home she dusted, peeled potatoes, and washed dishes. With the advent of electricity, she clung to her kerosene lamp, permitting the rest of the family to use the electric light in the kitchen, but the minute they left, she would turn off the light and use her kerosene lamp. Neither would she use any electric appliances. When Mrs. Cather bought a new electric iron, Margie rose at an early hour to do her ironing with the old sad-irons. She did not want to hurt anyone's feelings by appearing not to like the new iron.

When Willa went away to Pittsburgh, Margie understood that she was working on a newspaper. One day Mrs. Cather looked everywhere for a paper with which to wrap something, but she couldn't find anything but the Red Cloud weekly. In Margie's room she finally discovered stacks and stacks of the daily papers. When she took some of them, Margie cried, "Poor Miss Willie workin' so hard writin' all them newspapers and you're just a-goin' to burn 'em up for kindlin'."

Sometimes Margie would pretend to read the paper and would say, "I see there's a great big happen." When a special nurse had to come in to care for Mr. Cather during a severe illness, Margie wouldn't permit her in the kitchen and actually locked her in the coal room when she went to look at the furnace. Finally Jack, the youngest Cather boy, told Margie that the nurse had to cook special medicines in "Mistah Charlie's" food and those medicines would make him well. Then Margie accepted her presence.

Margie loved to investigate the bureau drawers and any luggage that guests might bring. She was painfully timid and having made an unfortunate marriage with one of the mountaineers who had come to Catherton from West Virginia, she was afraid he would come and take her away. When the Cathers moved into their new

house in town, Margie asked Mr. Cather to build a
board fence so that people on the street "wouldn't be
lookin' at her."

A professor from Yale once wrote Miss Cather:

Where did you get Mahailey may I ask? . . . With a
simplicity that reaches perfection, you have created Mahailey—small matter where you got her. She will live
forever—enveloped in a little sadness that makes her
characterization utterly beautiful. You have made impressions that are stronger than reality and though there
was nothing terribly important about Mahailey's func-
tion in that little epic, she will live longer than
Claude . . .

*   *   *

Willa had another circle of friends—people much
older than she, but nevertheless unusual persons whom
she admired. Foremost among these were Mr. and Mrs.
James Miner the parents of her childhood friends who
appear as "Mr. and Mrs. Harling" in *My Ántonia.* Of
Mrs. Miner she wrote:

I have never drawn but one portrait of an actual per-
son. That was the mother of the neighbor family in
My Ántonia. She was the mother of my childhood
chums in Red Cloud. I used her for this reason: While
I was getting under way with the book in the White
Mountains, I received the word of her death. One

clings to one's friends so—I don't know why it was—but the resolve came over me that I would put her into that book as nearly drawn from the life as I could do it. I had not seen her for years.

I have always been so glad that I did so, because her daughters were so deeply touched. When the book was published it recalled to them little traits of hers that they had not remembered of themselves—as, for example, that when she was vexed she used to dig her heels into the floor as she walked and go clump! clump! clump! across the floor. They cannot speak of the book without weeping.

Mrs. Julia Miner, born in Christiana, Norway—she refused to call it Oslo—had grown up with music. In Norway every boy or girl must learn a trade, even though he planned to enter a profession. Her father, James Erickson, had chosen boot-making, but his real life was music. He became oboe soloist in Ole Bull's Royal Norwegian Orchestra. As a child, Mrs. Miner had attended rehearsals and concerts; too small to occupy a regular seat, she was squeezed into the orchestra pit beside her father.

Throughout her life she retained her interest in music. Willa liked to hear "little mother," as her children called her, play selections from the opera on the new Miner Chickering piano and tell how Ole Bull used to rap his baton smartly over the knuckles of a musi-

cian who played a sour note. Mrs. Miner had a book
of opera in simplified form which she had first learned
on the melodion.

Often Mrs. Miner related interesting incidents of
her childhood when her parents had lived not far from
the Summer Palace. Norway and Sweden were then
united. On warm mornings, after she had been dressed
up, little Julie would walk around the royal grounds
which were enclosed by an iron fence. Once as she
pressed her face against the bars to smell some lovely
flowers, she felt a hand on her head and looked up into
the ugliest, most wrinkled face she had ever seen. "Do
you want a flower?" the old lady asked.

Much too frightened to speak, Julie nodded. The
lady picked two sprays of white German stocks and
with a reassuring smile handed them to the delighted
child. Mumbling her thanks, Julie ran home to show
the treasures. When she told how she had received
them, her father exclaimed, "Why, that was the Dowager Queen. The mother of our King."

Julie went to the school founded by the Dowager
Queen for young ladies whose fathers were employed
at court. Although she was only nine, the youngest of
the students, she finished during her first term a dozen
hand-sewn linen shirts for one of her uncles. During
free winter hours her father would take her out on the
bay to skate, pushing her in a *sluffe,* made like a chair

and fitted with runners. Julie loved Norway with its blue sky and blue waters, its long white winters, its high mountains and dark forests; but her father, a restless dreamer, had heard Ole Bull talk about America and its opportunities. (Later Ole Bull came to Pennsylvania and founded a colony of Norwegians, but it failed and he returned to music to remake his fortune, dying in Norway in 1880.)

James Erickson booked passage on a sailing vessel, ignoring the fact that his wife was soon to deliver a child. The trip was endless. Julie entertained herself with a doll given her by two aunts (Milliners to the Queen) and dressed in silks and velvets. Before the voyage ended, Julie's mother gave birth to twin boys.

A Norwegian tradition of the sea says that no harm can ever come to a ship on which a child is born. Therefore, doubly blessed, the captain planned a festive christening and dinner to be held the night the boat docked. The mother, not yet well enough to go ashore, could enjoy the entertainment aboard. When the musicians from New York arrived, Mr. Erickson brought out his oboe and joined them. Doubtless little Julie clutched her precious doll and was grateful that she had something to take the place of the customary affection from her parents.

Soon after the family went ashore, and while they were still in New York, one of the babies died; and although the other was quite frail, the family moved on to Galena, Illinois where Mr. Erickson established himself in the boot- and shoe-making business. While her mother worried over the sickly baby, who soon died, Julie had her own problems. As there was no other home available, the immigrants had to live in the same house with another family who had a girl about Julie's age. Although Julie understood only Norwegian she was well aware that the other child wanted the precious doll.

Julie wouldn't have minded so much if the doll had been treated gently, but when she complained to her mother, Mrs. Erickson told her that she must get along or there would be no roof over their heads. Not one to compromise, Julie rose one morning before anyone was up, stole down to the lower end of the garden where the thickest currant bushes grew, and there deep under the shade where no one would ever plow, she dug a hole and defiantly tucked into it the doll and all its finery. Smoothing the ground above it, she returned to bed. Not until years later did she tell her children the story.

After a time Julie's father grew restless and although he had many friends in Galena, among them a young man named Ulysses S. Grant who was clerking in his father's leather store, and from whom Mr. Erickson bought materials, he thought he could do better farther west. He moved his family to Iowa where Julie grew up, went with her father when he played the fiddle at country dances, and eventually met and married James Miner, an Iowa farmer.

Mr. Erickson liked his son-in-law and made him a pair of boots which so greatly pleased young Mr. Miner that he would never wear any other kind of footwear. When James Miner bought a general store and moved to Nebraska, the Ericksons stayed in Iowa. After Mrs. Erickson died, Mr. Erickson visited his daughter in Red Cloud and drifted eventually into Kansas to settle on the north branch of the Solomon River. Although he wasn't in Red Cloud long, Willa must have observed him well, for she wrote about a man very much like him in "El Dorado: A Kansas Recessional," "New England Magazine," June, 1901.

Mrs. Miner could manage horses. In Iowa she had a team of her own, and in Red Cloud Mr. Miner bought Topsy, a former race horse. Although Mr. Miner wouldn't touch the horse, his wife became quite fond of her and had shafts put in the buggy so that she could drive her.

One day Mrs. Alex Campbell, wife of the superintendent of the Burlington Railroad for whom Campbell, Neb., is named, came to visit. She was a quiet little person without any knowledge of horses and she thought a drive in the country behind Topsy, the trotting horse, would be just lovely. Naturally she didn't suspect that Topsy's favorite trick was to get the bit in her teeth and ignore any pull on the lines.

When the women returned after an absence of several hours, Mrs. Miner's blonde hair had escaped its smooth coils, her face was flushed, her body exhausted. Somewhat surprised at her appearance, the children inquired about the drive. Mrs. Campbell exclaimed, "Oh! It was delightful! Your mother manages the horse beautifully. Such spirit and such speed!" Although the visitor didn't know it and their mother would never admit it, the children knew that Topsy had run away and that only their mother's small, plump, but determined hands on the reins had brought the rig safely home.

Mrs. Miner's flexible white hands were symbolic of her whole interest in life. Willa described them at the keyboard in *My Ántonia*. Carrie Miner asked her, "Willie, what a strange thing to remember? Where do you store such things?"

"Why, when I was writing about it, it came right out of the ink bottle," she answered.

To Willa, the Miners were always doing something exciting—or at least, when they did it, it had a special color. Mrs. Miner made cooking a festival and visiting the garden an adventure. She did her share in making the Miner Brothers' Store in Red Cloud a success. Mr. Miner's favorite method of inviting guests was to tap on the center plate of the telephone mouthpiece (a private line to his home). When Mrs. Miner answered, he would talk to her a moment, then turn to the visitor. "Mrs. Miner's on the phone. She'd like to talk to you." This was the signal for Mrs. Miner to invite whoever it was for dinner. The telephone, still a new fangled curiosity in Red Cloud, was excellent advertising. People could scarcely believe it was actually bringing a voice from two blocks away.

Hugh and James Miner had started the first real department store in southwest Nebraska in 1878. When it was certain that the railroad would pass through Red Cloud, they bought property and began business in a wooden building, putting up a brick one in 1883. The railroad coming through in '79 brought many new settlers and hundreds of wagons passed along the Republican River. The whole drama of pioneer hope and fear was played out in the Miner Brothers' Store. The Store, whose advertised slogan was "Live and Let Live," is the first scene of *O Pioneers* and the building is described in *Two Friends*.

James Miner was the kind of business man who was willing to help those who he thought were worthy. When he put the business on a cash basis, he issued coupon books to carry his customers over until they could pay. The customers signed notes; the notes could be sold to the bank and bookkeeping was eliminated.

One day a short, grubby-looking woman appeared in the store, and twisting her rough hands said, "Mr. Miner, I don't see how we can make it if we got to pay cash." She was penniless. The family, with nine children and an invalid father, were crowded into a poor sod house.

"About how much credit do you think you'd need to take you through the winter?" Mr. Miner asked.

The woman counted on her fingers. "We got a pig that the children are feeding with pig-weed and grass. We got a little sod corn and we can use part of that to fatten him and that'll make our meat. The rest of the sod corn I'll have ground into meal. There's a little broom corn to sell and enough cane to make sorghum to last through the winter." She looked at her gnarled fingers a minute then met his eyes, "Well, if I could get twenty-five to thirty dollars worth of groceries this winter, I could make it. About all I'll have to buy is sugar and coffee."

"Don't you worry. We'll take you through."

The remarkable part was that she did get along on just that and there were many others equally frugal.

Not all Red Cloud merchants so treated their customers. For instance, the first grocer, to bring in bananas and grapes was so avaricious that if a woman sampled a grape, he would include the fractional weight in his price, saying, ". . . And for the one you ate."

[67]

Mr. Miner could be stern enough, though. One day, a woman came to solicit funds to pay a professional temperance lecturer. The local anti-saloon league quickly followed the influx of liquor dealers, gamblers, and prostitutes that came with the railroad, but this particular self-appointed crusader was neglecting her family for her other interests. At that time the neighborhood had local option—that is, each town decided for itself whether or not it would have saloons.

At her request for money Mr. Miner asked her how much she expected, and bridling a little, she said she believed a man in his position and with his responsibility ought to give a hundred dollars. At this he laughed mirthlessly and turning to his daughter Carrie, said, "Shall I give her ten?"

Then with flashing eyes he faced his visitor, "I'll give you twenty-five, but I see no reason why I should finance the whole affair. After all, why should I pay anything at all when I think the type of control we have is working very well?"

Actually Mr. Miner only entered a saloon to rescue some friend, but at his words the woman flared, "Well, if it weren't for men like you, we wouldn't have places like that for our boys to go."

Mr. Miner slid from the high office stool where he usually sat, and making a deep bow, said, "I can return the compliment. If it weren't for mothers like you, boys wouldn't be going to places like that."

Naturally enough, when a few nights later he found the son of this woman on the back porch making love to the hired girl, he was furious. He had already warned the boy against hanging about the yard trying to attract the attention of the girls in the kitchen. This time he forbade the girl to see him again. Just as furious as her employer, she packed her clothes and left. The episode is repeated by Willa in *My Ántonia*.

*　　*　　*

Another friend of those days was Mrs. Silas Garber, wife of the ex-governor of Nebraska, about whom Willa wrote *A Lost Lady*. Miss Cather later said:

A Lost Lady was a woman I loved very much in my childhood. Now the problem was to get her not like a standardized heroine in fiction, but as she really was, and not to care about anything else in the story except that one character. And there is nothing but that portrait. Everything else is subordinate.

I didn't try to make a character study, but just a portrait like a thin miniature painted on ivory. A character study of Mrs. Forrester would have been very, very different. I wasn't interested in her character when I was little, but in her lovely hair and her laugh which made me happy clear down to my toes.

A Lost Lady was written in five months, but I worked with some fervor. I discarded ever so many drafts, and in the beginning wrote it in the first person, speaking as the boy himself. The question was, by what medium could I present her the most vividly, and that, of course, meant the most truly. There was no fun in it unless I could get her just as I remembered her and produce the effect she had on me and the many others who knew her. I had to succeed in this. Otherwise, I would have been cheating, and there would have been no more fun in that than there is in cheating at solitaire.

Oh, yes, the real character died. It never occurred to me to write the story until she had, and there are no children who could be hurt.

Silas Garber, a captain in the Union Army, had heard from a Mexican in his employ stories about a valley where the grass grew as high as a man's head and summer lasted all through the year. After the war, in the spring of 1870, he and his two brothers, Joseph and Abram, traveled up the Republican Valley on horseback, past the stockade at Guide Rock to the present location of Red Cloud, and there Silas Garber selected his claim, and on it the site for the stockade—a hill from which one could view all the surrounding country where grazing buffalo drifted toward the river to drink, and deer made noiseless shadows in the swaying grass. Around the foot of the stockade hill twisted Crooked Creek

which spread itself in a swamp extending along the bot-
tomland down the Valley. On the hillside the Garber
party plowed and put in a garden, and returned to Beatrice, Nebraska, on July 17, to file claims at the land
office.

After the stockade was finished, Silas constructed, in
a bank west of the enclosure, a dugout with logs placed
against it for walls and poles braced across the top to
support the covering of branches and sod. In this primitive dwelling the first public meetings were held, the
first election took place, the first liquor was sold, and
the first organization of the county and the first school
were held. A widower with one son, Captain Garber
kept his own house, sold provisions and planned for the
town he was determined to name Red Cloud, in honor
of the renegade Indian Sioux chief who had been rather
a terror to the whites, but who in 1880 made a peace
treaty which he kept.

The actual naming of the town took place at the
David Heffelbower homestead on Indian Creek where
the men congregated to encourage David who was not
yet old enough to file his own claim, but who was so
diligent that he had won the cooperation of the whole
stockade. On a warm fall night of 1870, Captain Garber
and two others were sitting around David's campfire
discussing the future of the country—at that time everyone believed in a never-ending ascent to prosperity—

and the small growing settlement closest to their hearts. Although Chief Red Cloud had never, to anyone's knowledge, been at the town site, the men agreed to call the town by his name. Today the citizens of Red Cloud take pride in the fact that it is the only town by that name in the world.

In 1873, Captain Garber became governor of Nebraska, and not long after, he went to California to visit his brother, whose wife had a beautiful younger sister. She attracted the governor—she and her two sisters had been "the toast of the coast"—and he married her.

A pretty girl, she grew into an unusually charming woman. Slight, willowy, about five feet three inches tall, she moved with poise, accepting graciously the governor's dignified kindness and his lavish gifts of jewelry and lovely gowns. He treated her like a favorite younger sister. Her crowning attraction was her reddish-brown hair, so long that it reached, when she was seated, almost to the floor. She enjoyed having it brushed, braided and wound around her head, for it was always silky, never fuzzy, and lay in soft waves at the temples. Her eyes matched her hair.

Her manner was gay almost to agitation. Elusive and suave, she approached frailty—invalidism made one more interesting. She exhibited but one hateful trait, and that was mockery of those less attractive than she.

Sometimes she would invite plain girls to the house to meet a group of young men, just to watch how foolishly the girls would act. Her amusement reached its height when one of the girls proposed to one of the boys.

When the governor and Mrs. Garber lived in Lincoln, she was considered one of the most beautiful and charming hostesses of the governor's mansion. After the Garbers returned to live permanently in Red Cloud, Mrs. Garber frequently went to Colorado for her health; but when she was home, she entertained a great deal for her step-son. Willa was often a Sunday evening visitor or she went driving with Mrs. Garber and her friends. Although considerably older, Mr. Garber enjoyed the young people as much as his wife. The Garber homestead was one of the most pleasant and commodious residences in western Nebraska. A five acre grove of cottonwoods grew to the north and east, and blue grass sprinkled with white and red clover covered the slopes. The grove was a favorite place for picnics and in later years Willa said that in order to write well, she had to get up feeling thirteen years old and all set for a picnic in that grove. At one time she even considered buying and restoring the place.

Vestiges of the lilacs still remain. In *A Lost Lady* Miss Cather described the road as bordered with poplars, but in reality the trees were boxelders in spreading clumps and Miss Cather simply substituted poplars because she liked them and through them one could get a glimpse of the house. The east bedroom had a southern exposure which overlooked the valley by the river where the children gathered wild grapes for Mrs. Garber to make into wine. In flood seasons the bridges would wash out on Crooked Creek, and the family would be isolated until help came.

Mr. Garber founded the Farmers' and Merchants' Bank but with the bank's failure, he lost most of his money. He had been thrown from a carriage in Lincoln, and ill health clouded his mind. His wife was devoted to him and for a time he rallied and was able to retrieve some of his wealth, but he soon relapsed into mental and physical heaviness. Throughout these months his wife tried to keep him tidy and presentable. She entertained more energetically than ever, hoping his young friends would rouse him to his old activity. People began to criticize her and the gossips tore at her reputation, as indeed they did to "Mrs. Forrester" in *A Lost Lady*.

After her husband's death she soon lost the remaining money and with it, her perspective. She needed a man big enough to provide a background, and finally went back to California, married one, and lived in contentment until past middle age. After her death her husband visited Red Cloud to collect whatever she might have left.

In spite of everything, her friends loved the "lost lady." Willa often said in later years, "Wasn't she a flash of brightness in a grey background, that lady? Can't you hear her laugh?" Other friends remember her parrot, her kindness to the hired girls, her habit of stealing into the kitchen whenever the girl was frying chicken, to get the liver from the skillet and eat it.

When, after writing *A Lost Lady*, Miss Cather learned that Mrs. Garber had been half Spanish, she said she was glad she hadn't known it before. It would have made the story "too pat."

For the film rights to *A Lost Lady*, Warner Brothers are said to have given Miss Cather $10,000. She did not see the picture, the Nebraska premier of which was held at Red Cloud, Jan. 6, 1925. Friends in Red Cloud thought the film a fairly accurate picture of the Garbers. Annie Pavelka of *My Ántonia* exclaimed, "Isn't he just like Governor Garber!"

Arrangements with the Santa Fe railroad for the use of their cars for props in filming the story were made with Sidney Alden, whose sister had played with the Cather and Miner children, and who had visited summers at his grandparents, the Perkins family who lived across the street north from the Cathers. Warner Brothers also invited Douglas Cather, Willa's brother then living in California, to visit the set and meet Irene Rich and George Fawcett who played the leads. Douglas thought Mr. Fawcett bore an uncanny resemblance to Governor Garber and that, as a whole, the studio had done an excellent job.

Later in the '30's another film, quite unlike the book, was released under the title "A Lost Lady." Miss Cather was so distressed that she never again sold a book to the moving-picture industry, and her will states that none of her books may ever be dramatized, filmed, broadcast or televised or used in any other medium now in existence or discoverable in the future.

III

"My Eyes and My Ears"

People will tell you that I come west to get ideas for a new novel or material for a new novel, as though a novel could be conceived by running around with a pencil and jotting down phrases and suggestions. I don't even come west for local color.

I could not say, however, that I don't come west for inspiration. I do get freshened up by coming out here. I like to go back to my home town, Red Cloud, and get out among the folk who like me for myself, who don't

n this picture of Red Cloud of the 1900's, taken on Parade Day, the brick buildings shown are still standing. The frame ones are all gone, as are the board-walks and unpaved street.

Red Cloud's street car, horse drawn, went down to the depot south of town, then back to the hotels on Fourth Avenue. When streets were paved in the early 1900's, the iron rails were torn up and the whole project was abandoned.

James Miner, first cousin to General Phil Sheridan, was the "Christian Harling" of *My Ántonia* and the "Mr. Dillon" of "Two Friends." Mrs. Miner as "Mrs. Harling" was according to Willa the only exact portrait she ever did.

On the collar of Irene Miner's dog was printed, "I'm Irene Miner's dog, Ber What's your name?" Willa describes the picture of Carrie Miner (right) in *M Ántonia,* in the scene where "Jim Burden," grown older, revisits Ántonia.

ictures from the Wm. Cather, M.D., period of Willa's life. When her mother
as too ill to care for her hair, Willa got her first short haircut (upper right)
eginning a trend lasting into her second University career. Straw hat was a con-
ssion to femininity, but note the man's watch chain. Willa probably put the
V.C. initials on Union soldier cap which may have come from enormous store
: such treasures in the Cather attic.

In the cast of "Beauty and the Beast," given as a benefit for Blizzard of '88 victims at the Red Cloud Opera House, Willa is the bewhiskered merchant standing at rear center. "Beauty," played by Margie Miner, is at Willa's right.

Willa described the George Cather home, shown here as it appears today, as the "Wheeler" home in *One of Ours*. She called it a tall house with lighted windows. Actually it has three stories and about thirty rooms.

know and don't care a thing about my books, and who treat me just as they did before I published any of them. It makes me feel just like a kid!

The ideas for all my novels have come from things that happened around Red Cloud when I was a child. I was all over the country then, on foot, on horseback and in our farm wagons. My nose went poking into nearly everything. It happened that my mind was constructed for the particular purpose of absorbing impressions and retaining them. I always intended to write, and there were certain persons I studied. I seldom had much idea of the plot or the other characters, but I used my eyes and my ears.

STILL LIVING IN Catherton is a woman now past eighty, who has embodied all the characteristics of the typical pioneer immigrant. When Hilda Kron was about sixteen, she and her parents came from Sweden to Red Cloud. They intended to go to Oregon, but they had bought tickets on the Burlington and Missouri instead of the Union-Pacific, and the railroad ended at Riverton, Nebraska. Not long after, Hilda married E. J. Peterson, a young man also of Swedish parentage whose father had come from near the Arctic Circle to homestead in the new country. The young couple, eager to establish themselves, started housekeeping in a newly-built "soddie" where Hilda had no use for her lovely shawls, dresses, spreads and remembrances of another life, but must keep them stored in two old handmade leather chests. Well-to-do by birth, this girl was no pampered child unable to work with her hands if need be. Her dogged persistence, the unfailing strength which enabled her to endure hardships and mother six children are symbolic of what all pioneer women did to survive.

The men had a full burden too. Every minute had to be used in tilling the fields and caring for crops and stock; and if a team worked all day, it could not be driven all night on the twenty-five mile round trip to Red Cloud for supplies, and then work again next day. Many farmers had no extra horses, and men like E. J. Peterson, after the day's work, drove part of the way to the village of Inavale, left the team there, and walked the last seven miles into Red Cloud where they purchased groceries, slung them over a shoulder, and trudged back to their waiting teams. Other times, Mr. Peterson was known to walk the full twenty-five miles, swinging along through the draws and over the ridges, coming into town about nine in the evening and leaving before twelve, the closing time for the stores. Having purchased his supplies, which always included a fifty pound sack of flour, he would load everything on his back and start home, arriving there in time for another day's work. With his driving energy he built up the Center Stock Farm, leaving at his death one of the richest estates in Webster County—an estate still managed by his sons and Hilda, who is now forced through the loss of one leg to sit in a wheel chair. On her eightieth birthday, one of her sons asked, "Mother, can you still say grace in Swedish?"

"Yah!" she nodded.

When she had finished, Henry Lambrecht, childhood playmate of Willa Cather, offered thanks in German. Thus still live traces of that life which so long ago inspired Miss Cather to write *O Pioneers*.

*   *   *

In Willa's upstairs room on the north side of the first family home in Red Cloud, she made a refuge where she could escape the household, arrange her books, papers, and most important, her dreams. Other children, with the exception of Carrie Miner who was really an adult, were not admitted. When Willa went away to school, her room was closed and kept for her alone.

In that room and in Carrie's room endless conversations took place. Willa would say, "Well, now, what then?" and they would go into some new argument. It was here they discussed the possible profession and life of Annie's father before he came to America, and the ideas for *My Ántonia* were crystallized. Carrie thought he had been the son of a gamekeeper; Willa claimed he had been the son of a doctor. They discussed the other members of Annie's family: the little sister who was crippled and who couldn't go to school, the deaf brother whose attempts at friendliness usually startled people, the older brother who ruled with desperation because they were so poor, the mother who was trying to accumulate something for her children. They always came back to the problem of why the father had taken his own life. It was the first story Willa had heard around the firesides of Catherton when she arrived in Nebraska.

Annie's mother was the pioneer woman who always insisted that any visitors take coffee and that they use sugar. Apparently, during the first difficult years, she had come to feel that no one could refuse sugar except for economic reasons; and if her guests refused, she would put in sugar just the same explaining in a broken English that she had plenty.

After the mother's death, Annie's sickly younger sister entered a convent in Ohio where the nuns found that she made excellent bread, and they gave her more and more responsibility with the baking, and made her instructor of a number of girls. When new machinery had to be purchased and installed, she went to Cincinnati, made business arrangements, and returned to supervise installations. When she visited friends in Red Cloud, they could see no trace of the blight which had afflicted her early years.

Of those who pioneered in the west, there were mainly
two classes of people: the European immigrants who
for the most part owned little or nothing, and the Easterners who had lost property during the war and wished
to remake their fortunes. A group which could not be
classified as either of the above was composed of the
sons of wealthy Easterners, who, because they were the
younger brothers, were not going to inherit much and
had to make their own fortunes. In the meantime, they
lived on the monthly check from home, spent most of
their time in the gambling places and saloons, and were
known as "remittance men."

Miss Cather mentioned two of them, "Trevor" and
"Brewster" in *One of Ours*. Red Cloud people with
amusement recognized in these two fictional characters
some of the mannerisms of Codman and Whitney who
built a large sheep ranch east of town and lost money
steadily. One of them dressed in a "western" fashion
with chamois skin pants tucked into high boots. The
story is that when Miss Cather's book came out, one of
the men was so afraid his rich uncle would recognize
him that he wrote a letter declaring that Miss Cather
had fastened the blame on the wrong fellow. Miss
Cather roared with laughter when she heard it.

Of the same type were Lord and Lady Edwards from
Ireland who bought a ranch north of town, put up a
rambling dwelling and advertised that they would teach

young men of aristocratic European families how to ranch. Actually, the Edwards knew nothing about farming and their several young European protegés spent their time loafing in Red Cloud.

M. R. Bentley, the notorious "Wick Cutter" of *My Ántonia*, loaned some money to an old German, John Wilhelmson and took a mortgage on his cattle. John kept up his payments until according to his accounting, the debt was paid. The railroad men were flocking into town and there was such a demand for fresh meat that the old man set up some rough planks and a few boards across "saw horses" and started a butcher shop, selling his meat at a good profit.

When Mr. Bentley saw money that he figured he might get slipping away from him, he prepared to seize the cattle as payment for the chattel mortgage. The bewildered old German went to Mr. Miner and his daughter who loaned him enough money to go into court and protect his property. ("More than once they put their heads together to rescue some unfortunate farmer from the clutches of Wick Cutter, the Black Hawk money lender."—*My Ántonia*.)

Coming from Iowa, Mrs. Bentley had opened a millinery shop and made enough money for her husband to start his loan business. He was a fine-looking, dressy man with blonde skin, rosy cheeks and a persuasive manner. The first money-lender in town, he charged an exorbitant rate of interest. If a man borrowed money and paid the interest and a bit of the principal each month, he might find at the end of five years that he still owed more than the original loan. But of all his victims, perhaps his wife was the most unfortunate.

Bentley spent generously for himself, but his wife had difficulty getting enough for the necessities of life. Tall, straight and dignified, she wanted to live with some self-respect. She couldn't have guests because he would complain about expenses; and although she wasn't well, she couldn't keep a hired girl because her husband would either get her in trouble or drive her away. Once Mrs. Bentley tried to take painting lessons but hadn't money for canvas or brushes.

One fall, in great need of a warm coat she discussed with Carrie Miner the possibility of a wool brocade Newmarket, a coat with tight-fitting waist and gored skirt which was the style of the day. Toward Christmas her husband came to Carrie and asked if she knew the kind of coat his wife wanted, asked her to get the measurements and order it. The coat cost $80.00. Everyone was astonished at his generosity. At the first of the year, Mr. Bentley came to the store to have his statement itemized. The bill was about eighty-five dollars—the extra five for groceries. "Do you know why I want this account itemized?" he asked. "So I can go home and kick about it."

At about the same time an over-solicitous man in Red Cloud conceived the idea of bringing orphans from New York to work on farms. If anyone claimed to be a Christian and would guarantee to take a child, he could get one; and some of the unscrupulous took the offer in order to get cheap help. The orphan project didn't turn out well. Most of the children who came were in poor health and all needed some medical attention. Most of them got into trouble of one kind or another, or ran away. During this time the Bentleys appeared with a girl whom they named Venus. Rumor had it that she was really an illegitimate child of Mr. Bentley. No one ever knew whether she was an orphan whom Mr. Bentley had acquired with the specific purpose of annoying his wife via this rumor, or whether she was an actual relative. But within a few years the child developed some nervous ailment and had to be committed to an institution.

Sometime in her life of abuse and ill-treatment, Mrs. Bentley must have decided to stay with him for the money she would get some day. At any rate that was what her husband thought. He was unpopular around Red Cloud and went to Missouri, then to Hot Springs, Arkansas, where he added to his considerable wealth by gambling. There, one day, while workmen were repairing the road in front of the house, he shot his wife, then called in the men, pointed out that he had lived longer than she, and that her family could therefore not inherit from the estate. Then he shot himself. The inheritance of over $200,000 went to his nephew. This was "Wick Cutter" of *My Ántonia*.

While these people and others like them were not within the direct circle of Willa's association, she was intensely interested in them. Another of the community characters was Fannie Fernleigh, madame of a house of prostitution. She would frequently buy as much as twenty yards of satin for a gown. A story-book "madame" she had her standards of dignity and did not mingle with her clients.

When she came to Miners' Store to buy carpet, Fannie accompanied the girl to the second floor and insisted on cutting the heavy material, with a "You let me do that, dearie. My hands are tough."

One of Madame's girls was a lovely eighteen-year-old blonde who seemed to spend a lot of time buying children's clothes. When asked what she did with them, she explained that her little sisters had to be cared for.

The salesmen in the store did not like to wait on Madame and her girls, although they and various prominent business men were not always so proper, a fact revealed one Spring night when Crooked Creek unexpectedly flooded and washed out from Madame Fernleigh's an assortment of leading citizens clinging to wreckage of doors, windows and other debris.

There was a succession of madames during the early years of the blustering prairie town. One of the young men went away with "Old Ella." Some time later, the local organization of the Knights of Pythias received a notice that he was dead and a request that they bury him. They held a consultation and agreed they would arrange the funeral if the woman would not appear. "Old Ella" was left weeping in a chair in Miners' Store where she stayed throughout the afternoon.

One of the ex-madames was in a way responsible for the final disintegration of the Baptist church in Red Cloud. A business man whose wife had died and whose children were grown, married the madame and they went East to live. After some years they returned, joined the Baptist church and settled down pointedly to ignore the past. But on one occasion a group of several denominations gave a dinner and one of the most "straight-laced" members of a rival church was placed at the table next to the woman of questionable virtue. The former rose, went into the bed room, put on her wraps and went home. The scandal finished the demolition of the already-weakened Baptist organization. Having been brought up a Baptist, Willa heard full details, and later she admitted that part of the fun in writing

Song of the Lark had been in depicting the church enmities.

The Red Cloud Opera House was built in 1885, and thereafter when anyone of importance came to town to speak, he was permitted to sit in Mr. Miner's horn chair. This was a unique piece of furniture made for him by John Tomlinson from the horns of Texas long-horns. John had to send to Kansas City for twenty-five different pairs before he found those with the right curves to form legs and arms. Everyone but Mrs. Miner admired it; she declared some child would get his eyes put out on the sharp points. Fortunately no such calamity ever occurred.

Among those who occupied the unusual chair was William Jennings Bryan who often visited Red Cloud. Willa first saw him in Lincoln and wrote:

My first meeting with him was on a street car. He was returning from some hall in the suburbs of Lincoln where he had been making an address, and carried a most unsightly floral offering of large dimensions, the tribute of some of his devoted constituents, half-concealed by a clumsy wrapping of tissue paper. The car was crowded, and the candidate had some difficulty in keeping his 'set piece' out of the way of the passengers. A sympathetic and talkative old lady who sat next him looked up and inquired sympathetically: 'Is it for a funeral?'

Mr. Bryan looked quizzically at his encumbrance and replied politely: 'Well, I hope not, Madam.'

Later when Bryan went to Red Cloud to deliver the funeral oration for the Honorable William McKeighan, a man who had gone from dugout to congress, Willa, along with the farmers in wagons from all over the country, came to hear him. Willa, under the pseudonym of "Henry Nicklemann" in "The Library" magazine of 1900, wrote:

When McKeighan died, Bryan came down to the sun-scorched, dried-up, blown-away little village of Red Cloud to speak at his funeral. There, with an audience of some few hundreds of bronzed farmers who believed in him as their deliverer, the man who could lead them out of the bondage of debt, who could stay the drouth and strike water from the rock, I heard him make the greatest speech of his life. Surely that was eloquence of the old stamp that was accounted divine, eloquence that reached through the callus of ignorance and toil and found and awoke the stunted souls of men. I saw those rugged, ragged men of the soil weep like children. Six months later, at Chicago, when Bryan stampeded a convention, appropriated a party, electrified a nation, flashed his name round the planet, took the assembled thousands of that convention hall and moulded them in his hands like so much putty, one of those ragged farmers sat beside me in the gallery, and at the close of that never-to-be-forgotten speech, he leaned over the rail, the

[88]

tears on his furrowed cheeks, and shouted, 'The sweet singer of Israel!'

Miss Cather used Mr. Bryan as the focus of her story "Two Friends" and also in her last story, "The Best Years," in which a little boy, named Bryan after his father's hero, knows that because of his name he must grow up brave and unafraid of the dark.

Another interesting character of Willa's childhood was Mrs. Holland, the hotel-keeping "Mrs. Gardener" of *My Ántonia*. "Libby" Holland was born in Ireland Elizabeth Carnegie. At sixteen she was betrothed to a Presbyterian minister, but instead of marrying him she ran away to America and eventually married George Holland. In Red Cloud they first ran a restaurant, saved money until they could buy "Boys' Home," and remodeled it into Holland House.

After their three-year-old son died from diphtheria, Mrs. Holland went each day to the cemetery. All morning she worked in the hotel kitchen, for she was an excellent cook; and after lunch she would go upstairs, bathe, and rest. In mid-afternoon, she would call for her phaeton. When the man arrived with the phaeton and Puss, Mrs. Holland's white and roan pony, the lady would come out and rub her white-gloved hand along the pony's back. If the slightest soiled spot appeared on the glove, back went Puss to the stables.

[89]

After Mrs. Holland returned from a trip to Omaha, she couldn't rest until she had cleaned the entire hotel. She claimed she could hear a cockroach walking in the walls. And according to Willa if her husband took a drink in Red Cloud, Mrs. Holland would know it in Omaha.

The statement in *My Ántonia* about "Mrs. Gardener's" diamonds—"some had seen them and some had not"—was true of Mrs. Holland's jewelry. One brooch, designed by her artist friend, Mrs. Sill, had been made to order. Mrs. Holland like to loan a new ring to some timid girl to arouse the curiosity of someone else who might consider herself more popular with the boys.

Holland House fronted on four lots, a space eighty feet wide and one hundred feet deep. At the back of the hotel was a building with two sample rooms in case any two salesmen wanted at the same time space to lay out their wares.

After Mr. Holland's sudden death in Oklahoma, Mrs. Holland went to Iowa and later to Omaha where she ran rooming houses. Impulsive and generous, she found she was no longer able to work, and that she had let her money slip away. "Mrs. Gardener" died in a home for the aged in Omaha.

The home in which the Cather family lived in Red Cloud belonged to Mrs. Newhouse, a German woman who had an extremely original way of expressing herself. Her sayings and nicknames for people have found their way into Miss Cather's writing. Mrs. Newhouse, though she claimed to trace her ancestry to Charlemagne, had no use for so-called high-society, and when someone thought himself superior because he lived in the north part of town, she named that section, "Quality Knob." In *Lucy Gayheart,* Miss Cather calls it "Quality Street."

A sister of Mrs. Newhouse had been wet nurse to Kaiser Wilhelm, and Mrs. Newhouse herself, had been born only twenty miles from Berlin. Her father was a weaver, and she had come to the United States when she was twenty-two. She recognized the greater security of the new country, and as a staunch citizen, she hated for anyone to say the old country was better. When after thirty-five years some of her relatives came to see her, she was happy, but whenever her nephew complained, "Auntie, we don't do like that in Germany," she would reply with spirit, "August, if you think Germany is so good, why don't you go back. Nobody asked you to come here." She was of that sturdy stock who came to America planning to find it better and meaning to make it better.

At first Mr. and Mrs. Newhouse lived in Pennsylvania, where he worked in coal mines; but when he was injured, they started a little store. In 1878 he went West to visit a sister. Knowing him well, his wife said when he left, "Now don't buy any land." But when he returned in '79, he had invested in a farm and soon moved to Nebraska to work it, while his wife opened a small store specializing in yarns and laces. At first their daughter, Barbara, was ill from the change in water and her mother, home-sick for Pennsylvania, went East. But when she saw again the black coal pits and realized what future lay in store there for her sons, she returned to Nebraska. Although she never ceased grieving for old friends in the East, she cheerfully went about the task of building a future for her family.

Willa, during those childhood years was, as George Seibel said later, "a flesh and blood dictograph—eyes in every pore." She absorbed everything and turned what she needed into her life's work. And the lusty Red Cloud of the '80's afforded plenty for her to absorb.

SCHOLARSHIP

I

"To Know the Parish"

Of course Nebraska is a storehouse of literary material. Everywhere is a storehouse of literary material. If a true artist were born in a pigpen and raised in a sty, he would still find plenty of inspiration for his work. The only need is the eye to see.

THE RED CLOUD to which Willa came in the fall of 1884 was a thirteen-year-old village of about 2,500 people, the leaders of whom had great faith in the future of their community. They had seen the stockade of 1870 with its six women, seven children and thirteen men grow into the county-seat, a railroad town serving a thriving territory which extended in all directions even into Kansas, six miles south. An observer on the bluffs south of the river could see many roads, all of them crowded with heavily-loaded teams and wagons, converging in a continuous stream to the river bridge where they waited to cross.

The Lincoln "State Journal" in 1883, said:

No town in the state is better off in the line of churches and schools than Red Cloud and even the children met upon the streets show that they are the offspring of parents who understand the value of and know how to appreciate such advantage. Red Cloud is destined to be one of the foremost cities in Nebraska, in time, and in years not distant will be the leading town along the southern border of the state.

The prophecy of the Lincoln "State Journal" did not exactly come true; but Red Cloud, Nebraska, has probably been described more often in literature than any other village its size. It is the "Sweetwater" of *A Lost Lady,* the "Frankfort" of *One of Ours,* the "Haverford" of *Lucy Gayheart,* the "Moonstone" of *Song of the Lark,* the "Black Hawk" of *My Ántonia,* and the "Hanover" of *O Pioneers.* It is the village of "The Best Years" and the several villages of the stories in *Obscure Destinies.* Willa Cather lived in Red Cloud from 1884 (age eleven) to 1890 (age seventeen) when she went to the Lincoln State University. She herself said that the first years of one's life make the deepest impression, and she has relived those Red Cloud years in each of her Nebraska books.

In many ways the Red Cloud of today is different from what it was in 1890. Then almost three thousand people lived at this Burlington and Missouri division point, where eight passenger trains went through daily, and hundreds of people stopped for meals. Today the population has dwindled to about sixteen hundred souls. The main line of the Burlington now runs through Hastings, forty miles north. Early in this century there was a railroad strike, and the townspeople sided with the strikers. The railroad changed its division point, and today the old roundhouse pit lies unused, lined with feathers from the new and flourishing Republican Valley Turkey Plant.

The Opera House, built in 1885 on the second floor over a hardware store—the auditorium where Willa gave her senior high school oration demanding the right to research and vivisection—is now a store room, while the front space overlooking Webster Street (Red Cloud's main thoroughfare) has been made into an apartment. One can still read the scrawled names of Willa's brother and others crayoned on the stage walls; the trap floor for the tricks of traveling magicians is still working; and under the platform is a small cubbyhole still half full of coal. The oil-stained floor still bears the numbers of the rows where chairs were placed, pieces of old stage background and scenery still stand about, and the same family who put up the building still manage the hardware store.

Red Cloud, eighty years old this year, has a proud history, although the stockade of 1870 was never a military post; it was an enclosure 80 by 100 feet made of horizontal cottonwood logs so that the inside corners of the stockade could be used as the two outer walls of each corner house. The outer walls were eight feet high, protected from cold winds and prairie fires by a layer of sod three feet thick and a deep wide ditch over which the men constructed a crude drawbridge which could be pulled inside at night. Instead of a gate, the enclosure had one side built so as to lap and form a lane, and at the entrance the men took turns as lookout. They wanted to make it difficult for the Indians to surprise them.

Actually the settlement was never molested by Indians, but it had several scares. The men had agreed that unless a hunting party were out, the firing of a gun should constitute a warning. One day a member of the group absent-mindedly shot at some prairie chickens and scared the whole camp. To add to their fright they heard a bell such as Indians often used on their ponies, but in this case the bell was on one of their own cows.

Once the settlers became excited over moccasin prints which proved to be those of one of their number who having injured his foot, was wearing a bedroom slipper.

Another time the men saw someone on horseback along the river, and as Captain Garber prepared for attack and led his men down the hill, the strangers displayed a white flag. They were a military party escorting an officer from Fort Kearney, Nebraska, to Fort Hays, Kansas.

The settlers, however, did see Indians. The new community was west of the established frontier and in the middle of the Indian hunting area where buffalo, elk, deer, and antelope could still be seen. One day a settler killed a fat buffalo north of the stockade, but when he had it partly skinned, he saw more. Stopping work he rushed to call the women to finish the carcass while he pursued the game. The women brought knives and had barely started to work when they looked up to see several nearly-naked Indians mounted on ponies swooping down upon them. With yells and warwhoops the savages reined up and stared at the women who made signs to show that the Indians might have a hind quarter, considered the choice part of the animal. But the leader laughed and said, "White squaws much afraid!" Wheeling his mount he led the savages away leaving the trembling women to stare after them.

The pioneer women might have been nervous, but they were courageous. When Indians came to visit Willa's Aunt Frank, she was willing to give them everything they wanted to eat, but she, much to Grandmother Cather's horror, refused to give up her little black parasol. Aunt Frank was firm, and after Grand-mother had tried to explain to the Indian that Aunt Frank was her "papoose," the fellow patronizingly patted Aunt Frank and went away.

The pioneer women had also to be resourceful. When the men laid out the plans for the Red Cloud stockade, although it was already July and late for planting, they also plowed and put in a garden. For-tunately the weather that year was warm and rainy and the new settlement had fresh onions, radishes, lettuce, turnips and many other vegetables. When the men found wild plums, grapes, and chokecherries along the river, the women put up jam. Their first Thanksgiving dinner consisted of wild turkey, prairie chicken, buffalo meat, vegetables, mincemeat pie made of chopped buf-falo meat combined with dried apples some of the women had brought along. The pie crust was of flour purchased at Beatrice (about eighty miles east) and shortening dug from the marrow of buffalo bones.

At first the settlers had horses, but the Indians stole them as fast as the men could buy them, and soon the men resorted to oxen which were so slow they were no temptation to thieves. The cows were brought inside the enclosure at night, and chickens were cooped in, under beds, for once in the tall grass, they would be lost forever. The most popular animal, however, was the cat. "Old Abe" prospered for twelve years in his position as chief exterminator of the field mice which loved to devour the food supplies.

When the women first came they lived in the open stockade and protected their supplies with the canvas from their mover wagons. Soon, however, one-room houses of 15 by 20 feet were put in each corner. The walls were chinked with native clay. Tables and cupboards were made of native timber cut into rough boards at Swan Creek, a saw mill southwest of Beatrice. Benches and stools were made of slabs cut crosswise from big logs with smaller pieces wedged in for legs. Bunks of native timber were built in one end of each house by setting a post into the dirt floor and lashing buffalo thongs to the overhead timbers. Cross pieces were securely fastened to upright posts and strung with buffalo thongs to hold the willow boughs on which the women placed their straw ticks, buffalo hides, and blankets. Each house had one door, one window, a sod roof and a dirt floor. In rainy weather, the rooms were not cozy. The women frequently heaped their choice possessions on a table and put up an umbrella to protect them.

In the fall of '70 many land seekers, a number of them Civil War veterans, and buffalo hunters passed through the valley. All stopped at the stockade to get a meal and buy bread. Sometimes the women would be out of bread and would have to bake biscuits—as many as a tubful, for the hunters didn't know when they might again find a settlement. Strangers were welcome in the settlement which received mail only once a week —if a boy could go to Hebron sixty miles east. There was great danger in such a journey not only from Indians but from prairie fires.

One drizzling winter day a German immigrant came to the stockade to get help for his sick wife, who was in their dugout over the hill to the east. Aunt Julia Miner Jackson, one of the women from the stockade, followed him through the tall wet grass to a clearing where, in the cold rain, stood a stove, a rude table and chairs. Over an opening in the side of the hill hung a dripping blanket.

Pushing aside the soggy rag, Aunt Julia looked into the narrow hole, a space just big enough for the willow boughs and straw tick which formed the bed. From the rafters hung damp discolored bags of food. In the roughly-made bed huddled under a buffalo robe lay the feverish woman and her new-born baby. Glancing around, Mrs. Jackson decided that the woman must be taken to the stockade; but the husband, whether from pride or natural perversity, refused and Mrs. Jackson had to return to the stockade and hitch up the oxen herself. With careful nursing both mother and child lived, and though in later years prosperity came to them, the father remained as obstinate as ever. When

he built a large three-story house with modern conveniences, he locked the bathroom and the front part
of the house, keeping the key in his pocket. As long as
there were out-door accommodations for natural necessities, he did not see any point in "wearing out" the new
ones.

In the summer of 1871 the Jacksons built a story-
and-a-half log house, and planted a cottonwood grove
—grown to a pleasant size when Willa saw it as "Uncle
Billy's" grove in *Song of the Lark*. That same summer
the first hotel was built of logs with a sod roof, with
partitions and furniture of red cedar sawed by hand at
a local mill where two men used a five-foot rip saw in
a log pit. The hotel, or better named "public shelter,"
had a dining room, kitchen, bedroom on the first floor,
and sleeping space above in the half-story attic. Floors
were of undressed cottonwood. Food was largely buffalo
meat and fried mush, palatable only if one were very
hungry.

Many of the settlers, because of the shortage of timber, lived in dugouts or sod houses, and they made a
joke of having a scoop shovel in place of broom and dust
pan. The better sod houses were lined with muslin
overhead, and in some, plaster had been put on over the
sod walls. Even so, sharp eyes would often detect snakes
darting their heads out from the cracks between the
plastered wall and the muslin-covered ceiling.

[101]

Mostly these were bull snakes who liked to live near houses and enjoy the eggs from the hen house and milk from the milk house. Housewives would enter a milk house to be startled by the sight of a large snake curving his glistening neck over the edge of a crock drinking the cream. Although rattlesnakes seldom frequented populated areas, the women kept alert. Grandmother Cather, (like "Grandmother Burden") always carried her rattlesnake cane whenever she went to the garden. It was a cane with a steel point and a hole bored near the top with a thong that went around the waist. In reality, the hogs were the creatures who destroyed the snakes by eating them. The rattlers striking at the hogs would bury their poison in the fat where it could do no damage. In return, the hogs devoured the snakes.

The second winter for the Red Cloud settlement was severe with deep snows which covered some of the cattle who had taken refuge in ravines and smothered them where they stood. Several Texas "cattle kings" had brought feeder herds into the Republican Valley to graze and about four-fifths of them perished—a total loss except for their hides. That same winter a mother with her child started from Indian Creek (that part of the county described in the death of Lucy Gayheart) to find her husband who had gone to Red Cloud. Both mother and child were frozen to death.

In spite of the bitter cold, the well-built sod houses

were usually warm and many housewives filled the deep sunny windows with plants, a promise of summer. But that summer only brought wind storms which blew off roofs and ruined possessions. Courageously men planted windbreaks and timber claims. Even their festivities had strange interruptions. On the Fourth of July, 1872, while everyone was attending an outdoor dance, a herd of buffalo stampeded through town and broke up the party. Some of the men rushed for guns and shot one buffalo. Another fellow in trying to lasso a calf, fell from his horse and caught the animal in his arms.

By 1873 the men had to go farther west for the winter's supply of buffalo meat. While they were gone, the wild geese ate the sod corn and antelope devoured the melons. Civilization, however, was taking root, and by 1874 the land had mellowed with cultivation and heavy rains. Prospects for a good yield were excellent. At last they could plant wheat in place of sod crops such as corn, pumpkins and squash. And then, with no warning whatever, came the grasshoppers that not only finished the crop but ate the clothes from the clothes-lines as well.

That year the Taylors, whose story is typical, put in a small field of wheat, and proudly watched it grow with a promise of high quality and abundant yield, regretting only that they hadn't put in more. The problem was a place for storage, for they had neither granary, lumber nor money. Finally Mr. Taylor took teams and wagons to the timber and brought home loads of small straight logs which he and his neighbors built into a solid bin, using straight poles for a floor and chinking the cracks with wisps of hay. When the threshing began, they lined the bin with straw so it would hold the wheat, and when it was full, they stacked straw on top to shed water. Their task completed, they looked on their work with satisfaction except for one disturbing fact.

The wind had changed and the grasshoppers that had been flying over for several days settled and began to eat. The horses were so restless that the men had to unhitch them. The men were so uneasy that they hurried home to try to prevent their own personal tragedies. The 'hoppers settled about four o'clock in the afternoon and by morning there was not a leaf nor kernel of corn in the Taylors' sixty acre field, which was just in good roasting ears. They cleaned out the wheat bin, ate the leaves from the potato vines, beets, cabbages, turnips. They ate the onions out, leaving holes in the ground, and stripped sunflowers of leaves and blossoms, the new peach trees of leaves and fruit, leaving bare pits hanging.

The outlook for the settlers was dark. For example, the Taylors had twenty-two pigs which they had been feeding on green weeds and milk. Mr. Taylor decided to ferry them across the river—the bridge had gone out with the spring floods—and turn them loose among the oak trees where there was plenty of underbrush and acorns. In order to keep the animals together and nearby, he went over every few days to give them a little of his precious sod corn left from the previous year. (Sod corn was the crop planted when the ground was first broken. As the furrow was laid open, corn was planted by hand. When the next furrow was plowed, the sod was turned over the corn. Sod corn was no different from other corn and was so-called only the first year when the new ground was broken.)

About six weeks after turning the pigs loose, Mr. Taylor decided they were going to be out of danger of starving. But one night the Otoe Indians passed along the valley going west to hunt buffalo, and they camped south of the river. When the half-tame pigs came out to investigate, they ended up as pork for the hungry campers. The man at the ferry heard some shooting and sent a messenger to Mr. Taylor, at the same time calling across the river that the owner of the pigs was coming. By the time help arrived the Indians had broken camp and vanished with the spoils, leaving only eight pigs alive.

On the whole, the pioneers were inclined to joke about their disasters. The Red Cloud paper issued special stationery with a picture of a grasshopper chasing a man and the words: "If you don't catch him in ten days, Return to ——." George Cather sent one of these envelopes to his brother Charles (Willa's father).

Someone brought a jar of pickled 'hoppers to the county fair. The stores advertised: "All kinds of goods sold below grasshopper prices." But in spite of their courageous humor, the majority had to accept help from eastern states. The army sent men to distribute clothing and food. Some settlers left the county for good but some came back the following year, and homesteaders damaged by grasshoppers were given a year's extension in "proving up" their claims.

The grasshopper problem was not settled that year. In 1877 the Nebraska legislature passed the grasshopper act which stipulated that all able-bodied men between sixteen and sixty could be drafted by the road commissioners to kill grasshoppers. The men had to work not less than two days nor more than twelve. For failure to work they could be fined ten dollars and costs. The money was to go into the school fund. Since there was no plan developed for killing the 'hoppers, the unenforceable law was repealed in 1899.

Each year brought disaster, but gradually the land was tamed. Prize yields were forty potatoes to a bushel and six hundred forty bushels to an acre; turnips were twelve to a bushel; beets weighed as high as eighteen pounds, cabbage twenty-eight; squash weighed seventy-seven and a half pounds; cornstalks grew up to fourteen feet with nine feet to reach the first ear; and nineteen ears of popcorn on a single stalk was not unheard of.

The settlement had some of the graces of civilization but many of the characteristics of the frontier. Schools were scattered throughout the county. Discipline was reputedly strict. Snowballing was forbidden. Sometimes the Red Cloud paper carried reports of those who had not whispered along with the names of those who had not been tardy nor absent. Terms were Fall, Winter, and Spring. Some communities had only one term, or three months, of school. Once in a while a group of irascible fellows would run several teachers out before the community intervened.

The local newspaper tried to do its share in correcting the young people. The editor threatened to publish the names of boys he heard swearing; and when he overheard a boy speak disrespectfully to his mother, he wrote a long editorial reminding the boy that sometime he would stand beside the bedside of his dying mother and recall with bitterness his evil words.

Another opportunity for florid journalism came with each obituary:

Death had marked her for his own, but hesitated long to close the life that had been so full of sweetness to all with whom she came in contact. Down into the dark valley, over the cold chilling river, and then into the beautiful city where there is no death, where sorrow never comes, where the sufferings of this earthly life are transformed into the happiness and blessedness of heaven.

*   *   *

Red Cloud was, on the whole, a fairly quiet town until the railroad gangs arrived in 1878. First came the surveyors, the brush cutters, then the graders and track-layers. The grading gang was composed of one hundred teams and scrapers, and at the blacksmith's there was always a line of teams to be shod while at the four saloons the teamsters roistered and annoyed the sober citizens.

The coming of the railroad had a peculiar effect on the layout of the town. As the only land available for their track lay close to the river, the Burlington constructed the depot a mile from the main part of town. Those who owned property at that end of the village expected new growth to start around the depot. The railroad put up a large hotel, an eating house and a roundhouse, while property owners laid out their land in lots. However, the movement of the business district south to the depot did not prosper, and by 1883 two brick buildings were erected on the original town site, far from the depot.

Willa's childhood interest in the pioneer farm life

. G. E. McKeeby, Cather physician, is "Dr. Archie" of *Song of the Lark*. G. P.
ther (right) Willa's cousin killed in World War I, inspired "Claude Wheeler"
One of Ours, the novel that won Willa the Pulitzer Prize in 1922.

ant Frank Cather, G.P.'s mother, was partly prototype for "Mrs. Wheeler" and
.unt Georgiana" in "A Wagner Matinee." Willa's youngest brother Jack was
e subject of "Jack-a-boy" in the "Saturday Evening Post" of 1901.

The old Miner Bros. Store was built in Red Cloud 1874 and moved to the ba
lot when a new brick one went up in 1883. Either this store or its success
were the locale for the opening scene of *O Pioneers*.

The store had four departments as large as grocery and china section shown he
Railroads were still incomplete, and Miner Bros., a favorite hang-out for Wil
was the center of trade for Webster and outlying counties.

Townsend Studios, Lincoln, Nebr.

Willa's Graduation Ball gown in 1895 was ivory net over ivory satin, trimmed with gold sequins. Whatever she might say later about her undergraduate financial privations, no undue hardship seemed indicated here. Off to Chicago for the Opera, she bought an elaborate "circular" trimmed with Persian lamb, a boa for her neck and an ostrich-plume hat, considered a fashionable necessity. After a few months of the costume Willa found it quite impossible.

The house where the Cathers first lived in Red Cloud is the house of "Old Mrs. Harris," *Song of the Lark*, and "The Best Years." In upper right wing, facing north, was Willa's room, called "The Rose Bower." It was locked when she went away to school. The downstairs front room is where the base-burner stood and where "Thea" was confined during the illness described in *Song of the Lark*. South of house was playvillage of "Sandy Point," of which Willa was Mayor.

of the foreign immigrant was now extended to stories of the old-timers in town and she was to utilize many of their tales in her books. Her method of writing was to suspend the immediate thread of a narrative and insert a colorful, if unrelated, tale of the past. Critics have said that she used this device to give her stories depth, but it is more likely that she wrote her material in the way in which she had acquired it.

II

"William Cather, M. D."

THERE WAS A PERIOD in Willa's life when science claimed all her attention. If she ever had previously an interest in writing, she lost it for several years. In later years she recalled:

But I didn't want to be an author. I wanted to be a surgeon! Thank goodness, I had a youth uncorrupted by literary ambitions. I mean it! I think it's too bad for a child to feel that it must be a writer, for then instead of looking at life naturally, it is hunting for cheap effects. I have never ceased to be thankful that I loved those people out in the Republican Valley for themselves first, not because I could get *copy* out of them.

[109]

One of Willa's first adult friends, was Dr. G. E.
McKeeby, a graduate of Bellevue Hospital Medical
College, New York City, in 1868, and for fourteen
years a practicing physician at Lodi, Wisconsin. He
came to the drier climate of Nebraska because he was
in poor health, and began practicing law. Early in 1884
Mrs. Cather was taken very ill and when the old Red
Cloud doctor came out, he just knelt by her bed and
began to cry. Mr. Cather was frantic, "Can't you do
anything?"

The old man shook his head. "There's a young man
in town practicing law who is also a doctor. He might
know something to do."

Mr. Cather hitched up the team, hurried to town
and practically forced Dr. McKeeby to return with him.
When Mrs. Cather opened her eyes and saw the capa-
ble-looking, dignified man, she relaxed, confident he
could save her. From that day Dr. McKeeby practiced
medicine. Soon after, he cared for Willa during what
was probably a siege of poliomyelitis, and she wor-
shipped him. He is the "Dr. Archie" of *Song of the
Lark*.

Years later Dr. McKeeby again saved Willa's mother
in much the same fashion. He had left Red Cloud to
practice in Colorado Springs, and on this particular day
was traveling back to Chicago to read a paper at a
Medical Convention. When his train stopped at Red

Cloud for twenty minutes, he alighted and talked with the people at the station. When he asked about old friends, the men told him, "Everyone is fine except your old friend, Mrs. Charlie Cather. They say she hasn't many more hours to live."

Dr. McKeeby went to the train, collected his luggage and had someone drive him straight to the Cathers', where once again Mrs. Cather opened her eyes, relaxed at the sight of him, and began to improve. She lived for thirty more years.

Dr. McKeeby had an individual bedside manner. When he went to visit a patient, he sat down in a chair by the bed, reached to his breast pocket to take the tip of a neatly folded handkerchief, and holding it by the corner, he would shake it out in one sweep which filled the air with a hint of delicate cologne—or was it the freshness of newly laundered garments? After wiping his face, he was ready to begin the examination of the patient. Other doctors might rush about in the middle of the night clad only in dressing gown and slippers, but Dr. McKeeby always took time to make himself immaculate. With dark hair, piercing brown eyes and glossy mustache, in his beautifully-tailored clothes and hat to match, he walked with military precision, a figure to inspire confidence.

Sometimes Willa went on calls with him or with Dr. Damerell, another local physician. Once she gave chlo-

Wm. Cather M. D.

Red Cloud

Oct 1ᵗ 1888

Autographically expressed (date) ....

My Favorite:

Color : *Sea Green* | Poet or Poetess : *Tennyson*

Flower : *Cauliflower* | Prose Writer : *Emmerson*

Book : *Shakespear* | Composer : *Beethoven*

Animal : *"Cat"* | Character in History : *Bonapart*

Season : *When the Races Come a go* | Character in Romance : *"Tricotrin"*

Scenery : *The "green" shore of Crooked Creek*

Music : *A Squalling Baby.*

Amusement : *Vivisection*

Occupation during a Summer's Vacation : *"Sliceing Toads."*

My Pet Hobby : *Snakes + Shakespear.*

My Chief Ambition in Life : *To be an M. D.*

Willa of the "Wm. Cather, M.D." period comes to light in the album of a friend where she recorded early likes and dislikes. "Sliceing Toads" and "Amputating Limbs" held a powerful fascination, and she really did cut up toads to investigate their nervous systems and blood streams, though there is no evidence that she ever removed anyone's limb. While she had determined at this period to be a doctor, her love of books is already manifest.

The trait I most admire in woman:	*Flirting*
The trait I most admire in man:	*An Original Mind*
The trait I most detest in each:	*Dudishness*
The fault for which I have the most toleration in another person:	*Passion*
That for which I have the least:	*Lack of "nerve"*
The qualifications or accomplishments I most desire in a matrimonial partner:	*Lamb Like meekness*
My idea of perfect happiness:	*Amputating limbs*
My idea of real misery:	*Doing Fancy work*
There is always some one person, or thing, for which we have an attachment exceeding all other endearments in intensity. With me it is for:	*Books*
Of the various modes of travelling, I prefer:	*Walking*
If privileged to make a journey, the single place or locality I would prefer to visit, above all others, would be:	*Rome*
As a travelling companion, I would most highly appreciate:	*A Cultured Gentleman*
Shipwrecked on a desolate island, I would most desire:	*Pants & Coat*
The greatest wonder of the world, according to my estimation, is:	*A good looking woman*
As an inventor, I think the greatest service towards the world's progress has been rendered by:	*Cadmus*
Of the many reforms at present under consideration, I most sincerely and particularly advocate:	*Huge Bustle*
The greatest folly of the Nineteenth Century, in my opinion, is:	*Dresses & Skirts*
My motto:	*Enjoy, let others weep.*

"Snakes and Sheakspear" are her pet hobbies, and though she cut her hair and dressed as boyishly as possible, a "*huge* bustle" was her idea of feminine fashion reform and "*lamb like meekness*" was the trait she demanded in a future spouse. Willa always had trouble with spelling and said she expected to keep a dictionary handy to her dying day. "Lack of nerve," which she deplored in women, was an affliction she didn't have.

roform for Dr. Damerell when a boy's leg had to be amputated. Miss Cather recalled:

How I loved the long rambling buggy rides we used to take. We went over the same roads this summer. I could tell who lived at every place and all about the ailments of his family. The old country doctor and I used to talk over his cases. I was determined then to be a surgeon.

Dr. McKeeby enjoyed Willa because she showed the affection for him that he lacked. At home, he received only coldness from a once-pretty wife who refused to grow up. His daughter, who might have comforted him, died at an early age. One can imagine Willa (like "Thea") discussing with him what might have happened when, as the Red Cloud paper reported, someone had found a package of clothes weighted with a stone at the foot of the town standpipe and had made an immediate investigation to see if the owner had jumped in the water tank. The same paper carried news of a smallpox scare up the valley and an account of the pollution of small streams from the bodies of dead animals. It seems likely that Willa combined these impressions to make the water-tower incident in *Song of the Lark*.

Dr. Damerell, a native of Peoria, Illinois, and a graduate of Rush Medical College, came to Red Cloud in 1882, where he practiced thirteen years, becoming superintendent of the state hospital in Hastings in 1895, later returning to Red Cloud to practice. Having no children of their own, the Damerells adopted a little girl, and continued to take an active interest in other children. One family which Dr. Damerell particularly helped was that of an Englishman who had come over and worked until he had acquired 160 acres. His dugout was small, with only room enough for a stove, a table and a bed. Every year there was a new baby, and each time Dr. Damerell went to the confinement, he found a new little catacomb dug into the bank with a bit of mattress and some bed clothes for the new arrival (like the "badger-holes" where "Yulka" and "Ántonia" slept). Once when the annual visitation was twins, a severe rain beat through the sod room and dirty water began dripping on the bed. The father had to hold an old umbrella so that the doctor could finish his work with at least a pretext of sanitation.

One day Dr. Damerell purchased some chairs and was preparing to take them out to this family when his wife ("Auntie Damerell") came into the store and caught him. He was thoroughly embarrassed for he would never admit that he had done a kindness. Once he left his hat on the table at a rummage sale, and the ladies sold it before he noticed what they were doing. They were frantic until they had recovered it.

Another of Willa's medical friends was Dr. Cook, who ran the Red Cloud Pharmacy. He let Willa work in his store and allowed her to take her pay in books, games and a magic lantern. Once during her University days Willa borrowed money from Dr. Cook; but when her father heard of it, he was furious and immediately paid the debt, warning Willa never to do a thing like that again.

There were two types of physicians in Red Cloud. Dr. McKeeby, Dr. Damerell and Dr. Cook were allopaths, while Dr. Tulleys was a homeopath. Allopaths treated disease by administering remedies to bring about conditions or symptoms different from those accompanying the disease, while homeopaths tried to cure by giving, in very small quantities, drugs in the form of sugar pills soaked in the medicine which would produce effects in a healthy person similar to the symptoms of the disease treated, on the assumption that symptoms were not the disease but merely the evidences of nature's effort to combat it—the artificial production of such symptoms in a patient was helping nature. Further, the homeopaths had medicines for each side of the body.

When Willa's friend Mary Miner had diphtheria, Dr. Tulleys told her mother to keep her quiet in a room alone, to wash with soap and water and to scald everything before it left the room. When her mother asked, "How can I keep the other children from getting it?"

he replied, "Wash everything as I told you. Also cut a large red onion and leave it on the window sill. It will absorb all the diphtheria."

Onions were thought to be beneficial in various ways. When roasted on the red coals in the base burner, the outer husks stripped off and the juicy center eaten with butter and salt, the onions were supposed to cure a cold.

Willa's medical experimentation probably began with an inherited set of instruments for "bleeding." Back in Virginia, great-grandmother Smith had insisted that she be bled once a month and her son-in-law, Grandfather Cather, had to do it. Possibly Willa acquired some instruments and instructions from her medical friends. She was beginning to study biology in school, and her news items for the local paper, written probably as an English assignment, make mention of new equipment for the science department. People were shocked at her experiments but she replied in her high school commencement oration in 1890:

We do not withhold from a few great scientists the right of the hospital, the post mortem or experimenting with animal life but we are prone to think the right of experimenting with life too sacred a thing to be placed in the hands of inexperienced persons, nevertheless if we bar our novices from advancement whence shall come our experts?

Even a year in the University did not dim Willa's interest in dissection. The summer of 1891 she worked on frogs, seeking information concerning their circulatory systems. She advised her Lincoln friend, Mariel Gere, who was a science major, to fix herself a laboratory down at the "Lincoln Journal," which Mariel's father owned, because in a newspaper office there was so much blood and thunder anyway, no one would notice the cries of the victims.

Later when Mariel came to Red Cloud, Willa first dissected a cat and then showed Mariel how to make a chemist's alcohol lamp from a paste jar by using a wick through the opening for the paste brush. Mariel later went to Falls City, Nebraska, to teach science, and found very little equipment and a rather uninteresting textbook which had been used for several years without laboratory work. She captured a stray kitten, chloroformed it, and using the methods Willa had shown her, she taught zoology. Then with a dozen paste jar-lamps she began experiments in physics and chemistry, thanking many times over Willa's excursion into experimental science.

Willa's interest in science persisted long after she left Nebraska. When she was living in New York, she met Dr. Wiener, brother of the Mr. Wiener she had known in Red Cloud, and with him witnessed some of Alexis Carrel's early work in blood transfusions.

III

"To Know The World"

IN 1883, her first year in Nebraska, Willa came to
know immigrant families of Czechs, Swedes, Russians,
Germans, Norwegians, and French, and each heritage
of European civilization had its impact upon her. Upon
moving from the farm into Red Cloud in 1884, she
began to read Latin with "Uncle William Ducker,"
not a relative but a well-educated Englishman who took
an interest in her. Six years later, at the University, she
took more Latin and Greek, and during the summers
she and her brother Roscoe read Virgil. Evidence of
classical influences in her work have been pointed out
by many critics.

Willa's knowledge of French literature began with
her association with two next-door neighbors, Mr. and
Mrs. Charles Wiener (the "Mr. and Mrs. Rosen" of
"Old Mrs. Harris"). A Jewish couple, they spoke both
German and French. Mrs. Wiener told Willa about the
French novels, reading them to her and translating as
she went along. As soon as Willa went to the University, she bought a French dictionary and began reading
independently, but she neglected her written exercises
in syntax and as a result received several "incompletes"

in her French courses. Her teacher finally told her that, true enough, she knew more about French literature than anyone else in the class, but unless she did the exercises, she couldn't get a grade, and she suggested that Willa write a certain number of lessons during the summer. Willa did so and eventually received her French credits.

During her University years, Willa came to know the Westermanns, the "Erlichs" of *One of Ours,* who spoke German; and in Pittsburgh, where she went in 1896, she went every week to read French with the German family of George Seibel, who like most cultured European families of the day were familiar with several languages. Each member of the group would hold a copy of the book while Mr. Seibel gave a rough English translation. They read Daudet, Alfred de Musset, Gustave Flaubert; they despised Marie Corelli and Hall Caine. Mr. Seibel, an important source of information on Willa Cather during this transition period in her life, reports, in the "New Colophon" of September, 1949:

We felt that if we could descend to such writing, we could easily coin a million apiece. But the mere thought of such a sum was philistine, bourgeois, blasphemous.

Dorothy Canfield Fisher, whose father was Chancellor of the University of Nebraska when Willa was an undergraduate, remembers a Christmas spent in Pittsburgh with Willa:

There was talk too, wonderful, cosmopolitan talk. The Seibels were very cultivated people, knowing French as well as German. Willa went to their house one evening every week to read French with them. I had lived a year or so in France before this, so this did not impress me so much as their fluent German. Willa had studied both French and German in her college classes, and of course there had been professors at the University who spoke these languages. But this was the first household where she had come and gone familiarly where cultivated Germans used their mother tongue freely, as naturally as English. With her passionate appreciation of every opportunity for enlarging the horizon of her culture, she drank in admiringly the atmosphere of this pleasant, friendly home, which truly represented what we all believed about German culture, in earlier days.

That evening, I remember, Mr. Seibel, standing before that enormous tree, looked up at it and quoted to us a Heine Christmas poem. . . . It sounded wonderfully fine as he rolled it out in his rich German. Willa was enchanted by it, got the book out from the shelves back of us, copied off all the poem, and before I had gone on from Pittsburgh to Vermont, had made an admirable rhymed translation of it, the first translation I had ever seen made.

And that poem was accepted by a magazine, a real magazine that paid checks, was published in their next Christmas issue, with a full-page illustration of the Wise Men, their animals, their attendants and the star.

I still have that—one of Willa's first literary successes, very thrilling to her and to me.

In May of 1898 Willa visited her cousin Dr. Howard Gore, professor at Columbian University in Washington, D. C. Dr. Gore had just been commissioned by the government to go with the Wellman polar expedition, and was even then giving farewell dinners. Willa met many important people, and, as she did with almost every place she visited, used her Washington experiences in a novel, *The Professor's House*, but she was most impressed with her cousin's wife, the former Lillian Thekla Brandthall, daughter of a former ambassador from Norway to the United States.

Lillian was a cousin of King Oscar of Sweden, and she told Willa many interesting court experiences, sang Grieg's songs, and read Ibsen to her. The Nordic influence became evident later in *O Pioneers*, and particularly in *Song of the Lark*, which was built partly out of her admiration for Olive Fremsted a Swedish opera star from Minnesota. George Seibel said that the first time he saw Willa after she left Pittsburgh, she had taken Scandinavia as her fatherland, and added, "I remember mentioning her name in the Gyldendal Bog-handel of Copenhagen and being received almost like an ambassador from an Empress."

However, the language and the people which were to have the deepest influence on Willa sprang from France. In 1902 Willa and Isabelle McClung, daughter of Judge McClung of Pittsburgh with whose family Willa lived, went abroad. Willa sent back her impressions in correspondence, published in the Lincoln "State Journal." In these reactions and conclusions one can see the trend which was to lead twenty-five years later to *Death Comes for the Archbishop* and *Shadows on the Rock.*

While in England on this tour, Willa was attracted to the oldest ruins and spent hours sitting at the foot of the Norman tower of the old castle in Hawarden.

The temptation to attempt to reconstruct the period when these things were a part of the living fabric of the world, is one that must necessarily assail an ardent imagination. The brighter the day, the greener the park, the more deep the significance of their ghost of Saxon oppression, the more mystically it speaks of 'far off, old unhappy things, and battles long ago.'

The cloister is perhaps the most beautiful part of the building to one who has never lived in a Catholic country. Its utter peacefulness in the afternoons I spent there, the Norman wall with its half-effaced designs on which the eyes of unfaith gaze in bland astonishment after a thousand years, the rain that fell so quietly or the sun that shone so remotely into the green court in the center, with its old, thick sod, its pear tree and its fleur-de-lis, they make the desirableness of the cloister in the stormy year seem not impossible. Without, Norman and Saxon butchered each other, and poachers were flayed alive and forests planted over the ruins of the free holders' homesteads, but within the cloister the garden court was green, the ale went to the abbot's cellar and the venison to his table and though kings were slain or communities wiped out the order of prayers and offices and penances was never broken.

Strange as it may seem, the Roman atmosphere wherever it was found in England was that which excited Willa most. When Dorothy Canfield, who was particularly interested in Italian life at home and abroad, joined Willa and Isabel, the three of them went to see the Italians celebrate the feast of Our Lady of Mount Carmel, in London.

Here were undoubtedly the beginnings of Willa's deep interest in Catholicism, and particularly in its transplantation to new unfriendly surroundings.

The procession was a religious ceremony, even to me who understood neither its origin nor significance. Before one realized it one was all clouded about with mysticism as with incense; fire of some sort burned in one, enthusiasm none the less real that one had little idea what it was for. These poor Latins, undauntedly trying to carry a little of the light and color and sweet devoutness of a Latin land into their grey, cold London had done with us what a great actor can sometimes do. I did not see one self-conscious looking figure in all the procession. Never did a little boy smile or poke his neighbor. The tiniest child was able to abandon itself wholly to this beautiful experience they made for themselves in the heathen heart of the London slums. The police stood in double file along the streets to protect the worshippers from what stood without, and what stood without I know, for I stood among them: Gomorrah stood without, and Sodom, Babylon shorn of both splendor and power. The howling, hooting heathen London mobs: men drunk, women drunk, unwashed and unregenerate.

One of the high points of Willa's stay in England was her visit to A. E. Housman, the English Latin scholar and poet. Willa had been to Ludlow to get information and found the old files of the little country paper where his poems were first published under the signature of "A Shropshire Lad." From no other source could she have derived the style and sentiment of some of the poems of her *April Twilights* collection. She found one copy of Housman's book in the Ludlow public library, but no one there knew anything about him. She telegraphed his publishers in London, acquired his

London address, and incidentally stirred up local excitement in the little town where people began to come
and ask Willa what it was all about. His countrymen
were astonished to know that Mr. Housman's poetry
had been selling very well in the United States for the
past six years.

In answer to a letter from Miss Cather in the spring
of 1947, Dorothy Canfield Fisher recalled:

Yes, I remember very well that visit to Housman, now
that you remind me of it. Let me set down, as I write,
what comes into my head about it. It may give you a
detail or two more. You and Isabelle, back from Ludlow, had secured Housman's address—out in some
rather drab London suburb, as I remember it. As we
went out together, I remember your saying how odd it
was that nobody knew a thing about him personally.
This was of course long before the Housman cult. I
remember your saying, 'We may find that he is a blacksmith, for all we know.'

At the house, the landlady received us with a cordiality
which struck me as a little odd, and called up the stairs
(no, went up the stairs) to tell Housman—as we asked
her to say that 'some American young ladies had come
to see him.'

He came running down the stairs, looking very cordial
and welcoming—and was greatly surprised to find that
we were not some young-lady cousins of his from Can-

[126]

ada, who were expected any minute. (This explained the landlady's cordiality.)

But he was courteous, said with a neutral, British pleasantness that he would be glad to have us go upstairs to his study. That was a plain, rather thread-bare room, I remember, with boarding-houseish cheap furniture—not ramshackle, but not a bit good, and badly needing some wax and rubbing. On the floor was what was then called in England, an "oil cloth" what we called (I think even then) Linoleum. Rather thin. A rug or two, also thin, and somewhat crumpled up. I remember thinking as I took in these details, and looked at the thin, ascetic-looking scholar with his straggle mustache, that the whole setting and the man himself were just what scholars had always had and been, from medieval times down to Nebraska University.

The discussion with Mr. Housman soon led to the field of Romance languages and research—especially the studies which Miss Canfield was making; and when the girls were on top of a bus going back to their rooms, Dorothy was astonished and bewildered to find Willa weeping. At first she thought Willa was hurt because the discussion had centered on Romance languages instead of poetry. But the tears were really part of Willa's emotional reaction to the visit.

Her first views of France produced almost as much emotion. She wrote:

When we quitted the decks at about 1 o'clock in the morning, they (the Latins on deck) were scenes of chill and heaviness and discomfort. About 3 o'clock, however, I heard a rush of feet aft and tumbling into my ulster and mufflers hurried out to see what had occasioned the excitement. Above the roar of the wind and thrash of the water, I heard a babble of voices in which I could only distinguish the word 'France' uttered over and over again with a fire and fervor that was in itself a panegyric. Far to the south there shone a little star of light out of the blackness that burned from orange to yellow and then back to orange again; the first light of the coast of France. . . .

Above all the ardent murmurings and exclamations of felicity, there continually rose the voice of a little boy who had been born on a foreign soil and who had never been home. He sat on his father's shoulder with his arms locked tight about his neck and kept crying with small convulsions of excitement, 'Is it France? Is it France?'

Certainly so small a body of water as the English channel never separated two worlds so different. In the railway station here every porter was a thing of grace and beauty. . . . The cries of the street boys were musical. . . .

The next morning Willa continued to see France with eyes of enchantment.

The last of the fishing boats were dipping below the horizon. The purple chalk cliffs were dazzling white now, and our eyes accustomed for some weeks to the blackness of London, ached with the glare of the sun on the white stone and yellow sand. A little boy on the stone terrace was flying a red and green kite, quite the most magnificent kite I have ever seen, and it went up famously, up and up until his string ran short, and of a truth one's heart went just as high.

Willa's trip through France led her to shrines of men whom she had admired for years, and whom she continued to admire all her life. On a later and soberer trip abroad she met the niece of one of these heroes, Gustave Flaubert, and wrote an informal essay, "A Chance Meeting," about her in *Not Under Forty*. But her first visit to the Madame Bovary country of Normandy held the excitement of youth.

Late in the day we arrived at Rouen, the well-fed, self-satisfied town built upon the hills beside the Seine, the town where Gustave Flaubert was born and worked and which he so sharply satirized and bitterly cursed in his letters to his friends in Paris. In France it seems that a town will forgive the man who curses it if only he is great enough.

Heinrich Heine died in 1858, but on the day Willa visited his grave in Montmartre, it was almost covered

with bunches of blue forget-me-nots. The tombs of
Heine and his wife, Mathilde, were among those most
frequently visited there, and Willa felt that most of the
visitors were young—perhaps some of them Germans
sojourning in France. Of him, she said: "The melody
of Heine's verse never rings quite so true as in the
years that lie the other side of twenty."

In the cemetery of Père Lachaise she visited the
tombs of Alfred de Musset, Frederick Chopin and
Honore de Balzac. Of the latter she said:

Balzac's monument is conspicuously ugly and deserted, but Balzac seems more a living fact than a dead
man of letters. He lives in every street and quarter. . . .
He told the story, not only of the Paris of yesterday,
but of the Paris of today and tomorrow . . . until he
seems second only to Napoleon himself.

At Marseilles, where the sun-baked little island of
the Chateau d'If lies out in the old harbor, Willa found
herself awakened to the fact that she was in the country
of Dumas' Count of Monte Cristo, where, in her own
words, "extravagance ceases to exist because everything
is extravagant." Back in Red Cloud, Willa had read
Dumas' book to her brothers not too many years before,
and in a sense she felt that her excitement must now be
great enough to share with them. The Count's prison

she found as important, and "quite as hallowed by tradition," as Westminster and Notre Dame.

And yet Willa found something more—a sort of internal peace which she did recapture and give the world in her two French-Catholic books. Perhaps her feeling that Roman culture in Europe was doomed, influenced her to commemorate in the books its transplantation in the New World. At Arles, she found again a deep affinity for the Latin peoples.

The finest thing we found (at Arles) was a section of a cornice, perhaps six feet long, with a great eagle upon it, a garland in his beak. The eagle, the one and only eagle, here in the far corner of the earth where the shadow of his great wings falls, the one bird more terrible in history than all the rest of brute creatures put together. Above him was the inscription 'Rome Eternal.'

Yet they say that even the most remote of his descendants are doomed, that all who echo his tongue and bear his blood must perish, and these fine subtle, sensitive, beauty-making Latin races are rotten at heart and must wither before the cold wind from the north, as their mothers did long ago. Whoever is reasonable must believe it, and whoever believes it must regret it. A life so picturesque, an art so rich and so divine, and intelligence so keen and flexible—and yet one knows that this people face toward the setting, not the rising sun.

In the period between her first glimpse of France and the impulse to write *Death Comes for the Archbishop*, Miss Cather's perceptions and sympathies had deepened, and her desire to show what the French had done in bringing their culture to the New World, had developed almost to an obsession. To her it was a type of conquest, unlike that of the lay-imperialist, but none the less powerful.

Miss Cather herself has not said exactly when the resolution came to write of Archbishop Jean Lamy, the French pioneer priest of the Southwest. She told friends that she was first impressed by the majestic black-bronze statue of him which stands in front of the cathedral in Santa Fé. In 1925 she found a book, "The Life of Right Reverend Joseph P. Machebeuf," by William Joseph Howlett, a priest who knew personally Father Joseph, Lamy's lifelong friend and right-hand man. She drew heavily on this book, getting much from the translations of Father Joseph's letters to his sister.

Through an unfortunate oversight, Miss Cather gave no acknowledgement of her debt to Father Howlett, and after *Death Comes for the Archbishop* was published in 1927, he wrote her a gentle reminder. At that time she wrote a now famous open letter to "The Commonweal," telling of how she came to write the book, and giving Father Howlett full credit. She also sent him an autographed copy of the novel, begging his pardon and asking his blessing. Her novel renewed interest in Father Howlett's book, which had been printed locally on a small press in Pueblo, Colorado, and quite a number were sold. Miss Cather sent two autographed copies of her book to the St. Thomas Seminary in Denver, Father Machebeuf's diocese, with a letter acknowledging her debt to the earlier volume. Miss Cather's book portrays both the Archbishop and his Vicar so faithfully that it is almost biography instead of fiction. But the misunderstanding was apparently cleared up amicably, for a quotation from her book was used for the base of the bronze bust of Father Joseph (now in storage) which stood near the Holy Ghost Church in downtown Denver. Father Joseph's original altar and pulpit are still in the basement chapel of the church.

Her interest in the religion of immigrant cultures did not stop with *Death Comes for the Archbishop.* The idea for Willa Cather's other predominantly Catholic book, *Shadows on the Rock,* came to her when she found in the Louvre the diary of an apothecary who had served under Count Frontenac in Quebec. She took notes on the diary and from them reconstructed the atmosphere of 17th Century Quebec and the people whose courage had founded it and kept it alive. After the book appeared, a pharmaceutical society in Canada wrote her that a certain drug mentioned in the book was not in use in the 17th Century. Miss Cather had the ancient apothecary's diary to prove otherwise. People around Jaffrey, New Hampshire, where Willa worked on *Shadows on the Rock,* recognize in the book some of their French-New England neighbors.

IV

"Faith is a Gift"

BECAUSE OF THE sympathetic way in which Miss Cather wrote of the Catholic church, many people came to believe that she was a Catholic. She was not. She had been brought up a Baptist, but there are strong evidences that religious doubts entered her mind while she was yet a child. First, perhaps, is her school oration, in which she pointedly sets up scientific investigation against mysticism (although the developing hatred of change in her later years is a direct contradiction of this attitude). Other doubts, voiced by the rebellious "Thea" in *Song of the Lark,* surely echo Willa herself.

There was plenty in the new, raw prairie surroundings—the inevitable struggle and defeat—which brought questions to her unusually eager mind. Some of the clergy of those days (for example, Brother Weldon in *One of Ours*) were soft-muscled young fellows who tried to make a living in an easy way, or they were fanatics who drove men to madness or self-destruction. Three of her early stories ("Lou, the Prophet," "Hesperian," Oct. 15, 1892; "On the Divide," "Overland," Jan. 1896; "Eric Hermannson's Soul," "Cosmopolitan," April, 1900) show her bitterness toward religious proselytizing. She said that after ten years on the Divide one was quite ready to commit suicide. A common practice of the Poles when they were too discouraged to shave was to keep their razors with which to cut their throats, and the Danes usually hanged themselves. The well-known incident of the (Mr. Shimerda's) suicide in *My Ántonia* must have shaken Willa's faith.

And then there was the burgeoning 19th Century pettiness of some of the religious organizations. When Willa and the other children were putting on plays, some of the little girls were to dress as fairies and do a rhythmic dance. One of the mothers objected that dancing was sinful, and when she finally permitted her child to dance, she was ostracized from her church organization. At the same time "moral" enthusiasts were circulating a book entitled "Ballroom to Hell" which was destined to stamp out the evil of dancing. To the credit of the Cather parents, their children were forbidden two types of entertainment: medicine shows and revival meetings. Later Willa said: "Those who make being good unattractive do more harm than those who strive to make evil attractive."

In her essay on Carlyle written at the University, she observed that it was lucky that Carlyle wasn't a minister, for though intensely reverent, he couldn't have been a success:

The minister of today should be as shrewd a wire-puller as a politician. . . . He (Carlyle) was too passionately, too intensely religious to confine himself to any one creed. . . . He never strove to please a pampered public. . . . His genius was not the tool of his ambition, but his religion, his god.

Miss Cather's stated antagonism against missionaries to China may have come from her dislike of a Red Cloud girl who married a dentist and went to China as a missionary. When she returned several years later with many curios, linens and objets d'art, Willa suspected that she had acquired them by some sort of mis-dealing with the natives. She could not endure the exploitation of possessions and experiences when this woman charged for her lectures. Willa felt that the ancient civilization of China could get along quite well without our cultural interference.

The first story expressing this attitude was "A Son of the Celestial," published Jan. 15, 1893, in "The Hesperian." Another was "The Conversion of Sum Loo," in "The Library," Pittsburgh, August 11, 1900. But she reached the climax of her disgust in the character of "Enid," the religious hypocrite, in *One of Ours*.

Miss Cather found it difficult to believe. "Faith is a gift," she said; and she admitted that even her Catholic books were written out of admiration for a faith she could not quite accept. Perhaps her interest in Catholic missionary-pioneers was a latter-day extension of her lifelong admiration for all pioneers, all people who gave their lives to tame the wilderness.

The first member of the Cather family to join the Episcopal church was Willa's youngest sister Elsie. For a number of years others of the family attended, and in 1922 Willa wrote her old friend Reverend John Bates, rector in Red Cloud, that she would like instructions. On December 27, 1922, Willa and her parents were confirmed by Bishop George A. Beecher, of the Missionary District of Western Nebraska who had been a pioneer minister in the Nebraska Sand Hills. Miss Cather admired the Bishop and often said he was just the sort of man she could picture as the ideal Bishop.

She remained a loyal member of the Red Cloud church until she died. In nearly every letter to friends in Red Cloud, she included a check for the altar guild. She installed a stained glass window ("The Good Shepherd") in the little church there in memory of her father. She remembered him as a shepherd back in Virginia.

ART

I

"The Happiness and the Curse"

MISS CATHER's feeling for the earth, the grasslands and the trees of Nebraska was responsible for the flavor of her best novels.

Whenever I crossed the Missouri River coming into Nebraska the very smell of the soil tore me to pieces. I could not decide which was the real and which the fake me. I almost decided to settle down on a quarter section of land and let my writing go. My deepest affection was not for the other people and the other places I had been writing about. I loved the country where I had been a kid, where they still called me Willie Cather.

When she came back to Webster County, Willa liked to go out into the country, climb a hill and let the wind blow in her face. She resented any talking while

Attributed her best writings to the land she was born in or with and admired

[138]

she was remembering the sensations of the land—the odors to which she was particularly sensitive.

I knew every farm, every tree, every field in the region around my home and they all called out to me. My deepest feelings were rooted in this country because one's strongest emotions and one's most vivid mental pictures are acquired before one is fifteen. I had searched for books telling about the beauty of the country I loved, its romance, the heroism and strength and courage of its people that had been plowed into the very furrows of its soil and I did not find them. And so I wrote O *Pioneers*.

The impression of Nebraska which engraved itself so deeply on the young Willa may have been more sharp and enduring because in Virginia she had been more or less protected from seeing the actual struggle for survival. But in this new land of the '80's there was no hiding the poverty, the worry, the necessity for heart-breaking labor. Here pretense counted for nothing. Into the sod houses and dugouts she went and watching the immigrant women, sensing much of their background of old-world tradition, realizing how unfitted many of them were for the life in the wilderness, she put herself in their place. She became, with them, *one with the earth*.

This country was mostly wild pasture and as naked as the back of your hand. I was little and homesick and lonely and my mother was homesick and nobody paid any attention to us. So the country and I had it out together and by the end of the first autumn, that shaggy grass country had gripped me with a passion I have never been able to shake. It has been the happiness and the curse of my life.

In 1884 there were few roads in Webster County. There were indeed buffalo trails over the hills and along the draws past scattered dugouts. The ravines were alive with color from mid-summer on with sunflowers, snow-on-the-mountain, purple ironweed, and later, golden-rod. Willa rode one of the Cather ponies all over the prairie. Later she drove a team. She was interested in everything: the Bohemians who had to live in the schoolhouse until they could build a sod house, the ten-foot mastodon bone which was one of the first pre-historic specimens to be found in Nebraska, but which crumbled upon exposure to air because no one knew what to do with it. She noted the wild roses, seeded by the birds, growing along the edges of the plowed ground and the sunflowers which liked to fill the draws and follow the wagon roads. Sunflower-bordered roads, she wrote later, always "seemed the roads to freedom." She knew that in low places the farmers planted cotton-wood and boxelder, but on the high-divide put in ash

second Cather home in Red Cloud was purchased by Charles Cather after
la had left home. It remained the family home until Mrs. Cather's death in
i, after which Willa never again returned to Webster County.

iglas Cather stands on the boardwalk south of Miner Brothers' Store. The
e packing boxes were of the type used to construct the play-village of "Sandy
nt." The sidewalk is the setting for much of Willa's "Two Friends."

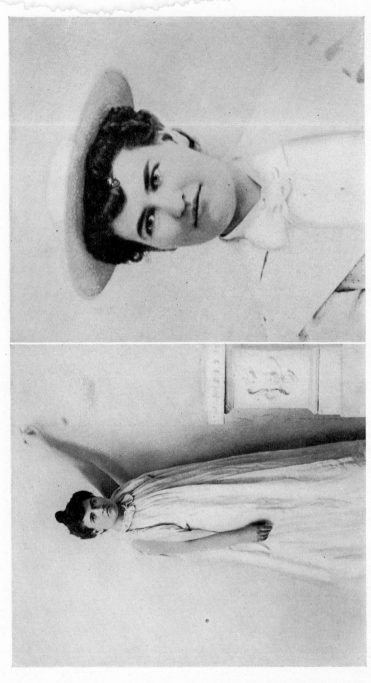

These pictures mark the transformation from Willa's long period of boyish hair-cuts and masculine clothes to a more feminine attitude. At left, she poses in a role she played in a Greek tragedy at the University of Nebraska. The wide,

st back from her first trip abroad in 1902, detailed accounts of which she sent
ck regularly to the Lincoln, Neb., "Journal," Willa is wearing her new pink
k Paris gown. Isabelle McClung, who accompanied her on the trip, liked to
lect Willa's clothes and see her dressed in the finest.

A harvest scene such as this one on the McDonald farm south of Bladen taken about 1910 is described in *One of Ours*. Today three men with modern equipment can do a job more easily than sixteen to twenty could then.

John Williams homestead in Webster County had a well-made prairie sod house newly-planted fruit trees (left) and the inevitable windmill. A house like this built in the county in 1898 and later cemented outside, is still in use.

In one of her books she wrote of an orange milkweed. After it was published, the Reverend Mr. Bates, rector of the Episcopal church in Red Cloud and an expert on botany—for twenty-one years a fellow of the American Association for the Advancement of Science—wrote Willa that no such plant had ever been identified west of Ohio.

Miss Cather was upset, but she had no way of proving that as a child she had seen the flower. She asked Carrie Miner Sherwood and Mary Miner Creighton to watch for it. "You'll think you see a basket of oranges," she told them, and she explained in what type of ground and in what season it could be found.

Although the sisters kept watching, they did not find it until one wet summer almost fifteen years later as they were driving south of the river. Carrie saw a flash of flame in a draw. "Stop the car, Mary!" she cried. Almost before the wheels ceased turning, she was out and over the bank, digging with her fingers a portion of the plant and root.

Turning the car, they drove back to town straight to the minister's door. He saw what they were bringing and rushed out, "Where in the world did you find that?"

When they told him, he could scarcely believe them, and he excused himself saying he must immediately write Willa a letter of apology and then prepare the specimen for his herbarium—an excellent collection which was sold after his death to the University of Nebraska for $1000.00.

Miss Cather felt that there was no place in the world with more beautiful wildflowers than Nebraska.

But they have no common names. In England, in any European country, they would all have beautiful names like eglantine, primrose and celandine. As a child I gave them all names of my own. I used to gather great arm-fuls of them and sit and cry over them. They were so lovely, and no one seemed to care for them at all! There is one book that I would rather have produced than all my novels. That is the Clemens botany dealing with the wild flowers of the west.

Miss Cather told friends that when she saw snow-on-the-mountain blooming in the Luxembourg Gardens in Paris she was so delighted and homesick that she could scarcely restrain herself from kneeling to kiss it. On her first trip abroad in 1902 Willa was reminded of Nebraska, and she found the wheat fields around Barbizon in France "quite as level as those of the Ne-braska divides."

The long even stretch of yellow stubble, broken here and there by a pile of Lombard poplars, recalled not a little of the country about Campbell and Bladen, and is certainly more familiar than anything I have seen on this side of the Atlantic. To complete the resemblance there stood a reaper of a well-known American make, very like the one on which I have acted as supercargo many a time. There was a comfortable little place where a child might sit happily enough between its father's feet, and perhaps, if I had waited long enough, I might have seen a little French girl sitting in that happy sheltered place, the delights of which I have known so well . . .

In the Provence, near Arles, Willa found the chill of the autumn in the narrow streets a "strange homesick chill," reminding her of the Nebraska autumn, "where there are geraniums to be potted for winter and little children to be got ready for school. . . ."

On the prairie, the new settlers found trees a symbol of hope, progress and security, a fact which strengthened Willa's natural passion for trees. She took an active part in agitating for forest conservation and observation of Arbor Day, adopted first in Nebraska in 1872, and later throughout the world through the influence of a Nebraskan, J. Sterling Morton of Nebraska City, Secretary of Agriculture from 1893 to 1897.

Willa could not endure to have trees cut down, particularly the cottonwoods. Once while she was visiting at her parents' home in Red Cloud (at that time they lived across from the courthouse) she awoke to the sound of chopping. Horrified, she dressed and rushed to Carrie Miner Sherwood's house. "You've got to stop them. I can't stand it!"

"Stop what?"

"They're cutting down all the trees!"

The two women persuaded the men to spare the cottonwoods. Later Willa said that for two weeks she couldn't sleep because she could continuously hear the sound of chopping. ("Lucy Gayheart" had the same reaction when she awoke to the sound of axes "cutting into live wood.") Another time she found men felling the cottonwoods that had been planted around the first Red Cloud hotel, and she begged them to stop. Finally the man asked, "Would you be willing to let us just trim the tops?"

Reluctantly she agreed, and one of those trees, the oldest in Red Cloud—almost eighty years—is still standing.

In Miss Cather's mind the trees and the pioneers were linked.

The pioneers feel that the cottonwoods are bound up with their lives. Yet everywhere the tall rugged trees are being cut down. Cottonwoods are out of date. The soft maple is the thing. I gave a talk at Hastings not long ago and made a plea for the preservation of the native trees. You should have seen the number of old people who stayed to talk to me and all spoke of how it hurt when one of the big trees they loved was felled.

A flat country like Nebraska needs great forking trees like cottonwood or poplar. The soft maples which have been planted in many districts to replace the hardier trees, live at the most only about thirty-five years.

Miss Cather charged that the American people were prejudiced against the cottonwood (the Spanish of the Southwest call it the "alamo") because it was no longer considered smart. She didn't ask for new ones to be planted, but simply that "the great trees that are dear to the pioneers" be allowed to stand.

Take the cottonwood, for example, the most beautiful tree on the plains. The people of Paris go crazy about them. They have planted long boulevards with them. They hold one of their fêtes when the cotton begins to fly; they call it 'summer snow.' But the people of Red Cloud and Hastings chop them down.

II

"The World Broke in Two"

Will

WILLA GROWN UP hated change—change in herself, in her family, in her home town, in the countryside. She mourned the old "board walks" which were replaced by cement sidewalks. She missed every tree that died, every landmark that had been destroyed. She was upset when she noticed strange children playing in the old Miner yard. "Carrie, how can you stand it? I just can't stand it! Where is that mountain ash? Did they destroy it?" Carrie explained that the ash had died and that so far as she was concerned, she much preferred people in the old home place. She had seen it dark and empty too long.

The question is often asked: Did Willa Cather desert the "grass roots of her childhood?" If she loved Nebraska, why didn't she come back during the last fifteen years of her life? The answer lies in part in the way she felt about change, standardization, and things growing old. She said:

At present in the west there seems to be an idea that we all must be like somebody else, as much as if we had all been cast in the same mold. We wear exactly similar clothes, drive the same make of car, live in the same part of town, in the same style of house. It's deadly! Not long ago one of my dear friends said to me that she was about to move.

'Oh,' I cried, 'how can you leave this beautiful old house?'

'Well,' she said, 'I don't really want to go, but all our friends have moved to the other end of town, and we have lived in this house for forty years.'

[146]

What better reason can you want for staying in a house than that you have lived there for forty years?

New things are always ugly. New clothes are always ugly. A prima donna will never wear a new gown upon the stage. She wears it first around her apartment until it shapes itself to her figure; or if she hasn't time to do that, she hires an understudy to wear it. A house can never be beautiful until it has been lived in for a long time. An old house built in miserable taste is more beautiful than a new house built and furnished in correct taste.

The beauty lies in the associations that cluster around it, the way in which the house has fitted itself to the people.

stop

Miss Cather talked of buying a place and settling in Nebraska, but she found it easier to write of Nebraska when she was away from it. When, after the death of her parents, she had the opportunity to take over the Cather home place, she refused, and when some years later it was given to the city of Red Cloud for a hospital, Miss Cather sent a generous contribution. Her friends assured her that no trees nor shrubs would be cut, and she seemed content.

After leaving it in 1896 Willa never returned to Webster County permanently, and after the death of her mother in 1931, she didn't go back at all. Her father had died in 1927, and with her mother's passing, there was no one of her family left in Red Cloud. It is little wonder that she could not bear the thought of seeing it again. "The world broke in two about 1920," she said, "and I belonged to the former half." The feeling was deepened by her impression that the second and third generation of Nebraskans were ashamed of their pioneer parents—of the calloused hands, the babushkas over their heads, their hesitating and broken speech. She felt they were getting away from the realities and said so.

All the farmers' sons and daughters seem to want to get into the professions where they think they may find a soft place. 'I'm sure not going to work the way the old man did,' seems to be the slogan of today. Soon only the Swedes and Germans will be left to uphold the prosperity of the country.

This rage for newness and conventionality is one of the things which I deplore in the present-day Nebraska.

The second is the prevalence of a superficial culture. The women who run about from one culture club to another studying Italian art out of a textbook and an encyclopedia and believing that they are learning something about it by memorizing a string of facts, are fatal to the spirit of art. The Negro boy who plays by ear on his fiddle airs from 'Traviata' without knowing what he is playing, or why he likes it, has more real understanding of Italian art than these esthetic creatures with a

Art

head and a larynx, and no organs that they get any use of except to reel you off the life of Leonardo da Vinci.

She felt that change and progress were not at all related, and some of her attitudes gave rise to the opinion that she believed herself to belong to some special aristocracy. As Robert Frost once said: "With Carl Sanburg, it was 'the people, yes.' With Willa Cather, it was 'the people, no.'" In France, although she found no difficulty in rhapsodizing over the peasants in the field, who "grew to look more and more as Millet painted them, warped and bowed and heavy," she was singularly irritated when these self-same noble "but unwashed" peasants left their field to crowd in beside her in a third-class railway carriage:

There were eight women and one wretched infant in our compartment, most of them women of the people and of the soil. Those women of the soil are all very well in pictures by Millet or Bastien-Lepage but they are not the most desirable traveling companions in a little compartment, on a burning August day when the mistral is blowing and white dust hangs heavy on the olive and fig trees. The baby had not much more clothing on than an infant Bacchus, and its mother was so tired and hot and discouraged with life that she threw the infant upon me and my dress suitcase and left it to its own devices. . . . At the end of four hours the guard called Avignon, the signal for our release . . . from the infant Bacchus who was cutting his teeth and had by this time nearly eaten the straps off my suitcase. O what a thing is a good hotel at the end of a weary journey, a journey full of heat and dust and hungry French fleas and people that are more distasteful than them all.

* * *

She said in New York, in 1925:

I like horses better than automobiles and I think fewer and better books would be a great improvement. I think it is a great misfortune for everyone to have the chance to write—to have the chance to read, for that matter: A little culture makes lazy handiwork, and handiwork is a beautiful education in itself, and something real. Good carpentry, good weaving, all the handicrafts were much sounder forms of education than what the people are getting now.

One sad feature of modern education is that the hand is so little trained among the people who have to earn their daily bread, and the head so superficially and poorly educated. The one education which amounts to anything is learning how to do something well whether it is to make a bookcase or write a book. If I could get a carpenter to make me some good bookcases, I would have as much respect for him as I have for the people whose books I want to put on them. Making something well is the principal end of education. I wish we could go back, but I am afraid we are only going to become more and more mechanical.

[150]

The fact is that for a long time in her New York apartment, near Mr. Henry James' Washington Square, Willa used kerosene lamps and fireplaces, having, during the shortages of the first world war, to go out herself with a wheelbarrow to get coal.

The same temperament which rebelled against change caused her to draw closer and closer to her small circle of friends, and to include few new ones. The last several years of her life she was in very poor health, but she did not want anyone to know it. She seemed to feel there was something disgraceful about sickness and old age. She wrote friends that if she could not move about with her old vitality, she would rather not live at all.

The way in which Miss Cather clung to those early years of experiences of her life has perhaps been best explained by Dorothy Canfield Fisher:

She felt, and said in print several times, and often in conversation, that for her the only part of life which made a real impression on her imagination and emotion was what happened to her before the age of twenty. This is especially noticeable, for most novelists have the opposite feeling, that the longer they live the more deeply they feel and understand human life. I have always attributed this feeling of Willa's to the fact that she was in many ways a poet, not a prose writer. She was deeply interested in writing poetry in her youth, and I have always felt that in temperament and gifts in many ways the most beautiful part of her work is the poetic quality. Now poets always—or nearly always—have this feeling of Willa's that what happened to them in their youth when the *emotional* impact was strong and fresh and new, was much the most important part of their experience of human life.

III

"Song of the Lark"

MR. GEORGE SEIBEL, a thoroughly musical German-American who knew Willa from the time she went to Pittsburgh, has pointed out from his observations that Willa's interest was not in music itself, but in. the personalities connected with it; that she could not play any instrument, read music nor sing; that her apparent interest in music was really always confined to performers of music or to music connected with theatricals, as in the opera.

Probably the first serious music Willa heard was at the Miner home, and soon thereafter, she had the opportunity to take lessons of a Professor Shindelmeisser, an old German who had wandered into town from no-where, and who often came to the Miners to talk about the old country and to practice on their new Chickering. He was a heavy drinker and many people thought he was unfit to teach their children. The gossips inventively conjectured that he had taught in some girls' school and had lost his job because of his affinity for the bottle.

Mrs. Miner recognized him as a musician of talent such as seldom is encountered in small towns. She wanted her children to have the best instruction and she always took time to sit with them during their lessons, intending to discredit any tales to the effect that he went about giving lessons while intoxicated. Willa put Professor Shindelmeisser into *Song of the Lark* as "Professor Wunsch."

On the day for music lessons, the professor stopped first at the Cathers'. Although "Willie" hungered to hear music and stories about it, she did not want to play and she would interrupt her lesson constantly with questions about the cities, the customs, the languages of the old country. By the time her hour was finished, the poor old man would be exhausted and exasperated.

He would go over to the Miners, where Mary and her mother waited. Bursting in and sinking into a chair, he would exclaim, "Vat vill I do mit dat Villie Cader? Her folks vants her to haf some music, but all she vants to do is sit on mine lap und ask qvestions!" He would shake his head and wring his hands, "Mein Gott! Dat Villie Cader vill drife me crazy yet! Qvestions! Qvestions! Alvays qvestions! I don't know vat I do mit dat child." He would cast his troubled glance on Mary and say, "Ach, Mary, come here yet und sit on my lap vunce." Her quietness would calm him and after a while he would be ready to hear her lesson.

Finally Professor Shindelmeisser decided to talk with Willa's mother and tell her that the girl wasn't learning anything about playing the piano. Mrs. Cather listened to his story and then told him to come twice as often because, whereas Willa wasn't learning like the other children, she was listening to him play and getting a great deal from his discussions.

During these years Red Cloud often heard the wandering Italian minstrels from Cripple Creek mines in Colorado. They traveled on foot in pairs, carrying their harp and violin and leading a dancing bear caught and trained in the Rockies. The first time they came to Red Cloud, a severe storm came up and the men, leaving their bear in an open corral, headed for shelter. When Mrs. Miner heard about the bear, she put on her raincoat, tied a scarf over her head, and went after the Italians. She told them if they didn't find shelter for the animal, she would have them put in jail. The men hurried to find a stable, and thereafter whenever they were in town, they managed to serenade Mrs. Miner.

The minstrels always played opera on their highly polished, perfectly tuned instruments; and they chanted a weird melody only when they wished the bear to dance. The young men of the village frequently persuaded the musicians to stay over for a Bowery Dance —especially if the date fell near the Fourth of July. For a Bowery Dance the boys constructed a platform and covered the top with fresh, green willows cut near the river, forming a bowery which was beautiful but not waterproof. Miss Cather mentioned the Vanni's dance pavilion in *My Ántonia*.

Years later when a friend was visiting Willa in New York, the two went for a ferry ride on the river. On the boat was an old Italian playing many familiar operas on his accordion. When the ferry docked, Willa said, "Do you mind if we stay on for another trip? I do enjoy that music."

Another musical event in Red Cloud was the visit of Blind Boone. He always stayed at the Holland House where he was treated with every consideration. Mrs. Holland did not go out evenings; and therefore, Boone gave special concerts for her and her guests, who listened eagerly to the heavy black man rocking back and forth constantly, bringing unbelievably sweet melodies from the keyboard. Willa blends him and Blind Tom in "Blind D'Arnault" of *My Ántonia*.

When Willa went to the University of Nebraska, she became acquainted with Dr. Tyndale, music critic for the Lincoln State Journal. He took Willa to all the concerts, and told her stories about the artists he had known. He had been a drummer boy in the Civil War, had later become a surgeon, and traveled with the Seventh Cavalry.

Lincoln had some excellent visiting artists in those days, and occasionally Willa went to Chicago to hear opera. She overdid it in the spring of 1895, when she stayed for a week and went to the opera every night. The last evening she was so exhausted that she fell asleep during Myerbeer's "The Huguenots," a lively opera with many drums. When she returned to Lincoln, she was ill for some time with what was then called "Typhoid-pneumonia!"

In Pittsburgh she had the opportunity to hear all the best music, and she came to know Ethelbert Nevin, whom she considered the "prince of them all." (See "The Man Who Wrote Narcissus," "Ladies' Home Journal," November 1900). His "La Lune Blanche" was dedicated to Miss Cather. She had visited at his Queen Anne's lodge, and once he had gone shopping with her, carried her bundles, and bought her a large bunch of violets. He appears as the gifted brother, the mother's favorite, in "A Death in the Desert" and possibly as "Uncle Valentine," "Woman's Home Companion," February and March, 1925, a misunderstood genius with a materialistic wife.

It was through Mr. Nevin that Willa met Isabelle

McClung who was to become such a close friend and with whom Willa was to go abroad in 1902. When Isabelle married Jan Hambourg, the musician, Willa was very lonely. But when she got to know Jan well, she became very fond of him and dedicated two of her books to him.

The story is told that once when Jan and his musician friends were spending a few days playing for their own enjoyment, Willa went to visit the Hambourgs. There she met Ysaÿe, the great Belgian violinist. When Willa commented on some medal he was wearing, he went to his room, brought a sackful of medals and jewels, and handed them to Willa who sat down in the middle of the floor, emptied the sack and began admiring the gifts from many of the rulers and wealthy persons of Europe.

Willa built the character "David Gerhardt" in *One of Ours* from a musician, David Hockstein, who was killed in the Argonne, Nov. 10, 1918.

It's not a portrait, it's not even an impressionist sketch of him, for I met him in all just three times. But if I hadn't met him those three times Claude Wheeler's friend and fellow officer would certainly have been another person, he wouldn't have been a David Gerhardt, he probably wouldn't have been a violinist.

In the days when I met David Hockstein I was not writing *One of Ours*. I was busy writing *My Ántonia,* and this latest book of mine was no more in my thoughts than it is in yours . . . But when I came to that part of the story, it was the figure of Hockstein, whom I had known so little, that walked into my study and stood beside my desk . . . Lately several of them (Hockstein's comrades), non-commissioned officers, have taken a good deal of trouble to look me up and arrange an interview, merely to ask me whether Hockstein 'amounted to much' as a violinist. . . .

One of the sweetest friendships of Miss Cather's mature years was that which she formed with the Menuhin family whose three talented children found a special place in her heart. She would go sledding with them in Central Park, and nothing pleased her more than a quiet evening in their apartment where no intrusions marred their quiet family life.

IV

"Desire in Art"

PERHAPS WILLA's first ideas of artists were formed around Peorianna Bogardus Sill, of Red Cloud, whose lawyer-father was a friend of Daniel Webster, and whose mother, a relative of Washington Irving, traced her ancestry to the royal family of Holland. Mrs. Sill, in her long, old-gold velvet gown, her diamonds sparkling, used to conduct cantatas or supervise her students in a musical "soiree" at the Garbers or Miners, and she must have seemed queerly out of setting in the little pioneer town.

Her parents, Mr. and Mrs. John Bogardus, already middle-aged, had pioneered in Illinois where Mrs. Bogardus ailing all the time and not knowing what was wrong, finally gave birth to a premature sickly girl who grew into a healthy woman. Born in Peoria and named for that town where her father had his land grant, she went to school at the Emma Willard Seminary in Troy, New York. But before she had graduated, both her parents died and at sixteen she married her guardian, Calvin Sill, a man much older than she. At her wedding, Washington Irving presented her with a pair of exquisite tear-drop earrings, made, so the story goes, from jewels formerly belonging to Queen Isabella (Irving had been minister to Spain). The pendant of the tear-drop was at least three carats and the square diamond above it of one carat. At that time people still wore diamonds as a symbol of success, and Willa was surely not unimpressed. Some of the performers in *The Troll Garden*, her first book of short stories, are reminiscent of Mrs. Sill.

After her marriage Mrs. Sill completed her education

and studied art abroad for fifteen years, and became so skillful, it was said, that her copies of old masters could scarcely be told from the originals. So great was her reputation, according to her obituary, that the Queen of Italy gave her permission to paint the Bay of Naples from her boudoir window.

While in Europe Mrs. Sill also showed such a great talent for music that she was accepted as a student by Arthur Rubenstein. She spoke several languages and after leaving Red Cloud, conducted a class in conversational French in Omaha, where she was associated with Professor McCarthy of Creighton University and Mrs. Borglum, mother of Gutzon Borglum, the sculptor.

It is not exactly clear why the Sills ever came West. Perhaps they were inspired by Washington Irving's "Tour of the Prairies." Certainly they were as incongruous in Red Cloud as Ruggles ever was in Red Gap. Mr. Sill, onetime owner of a clothing business in Troy, had spent a fortune keeping his young wife abroad. Neither was overly practical and Mrs. Sill had no understanding whatever of the value of money. When they planned to come West, perhaps to get a fresh start in a new land, Mrs. Sill had a number of silver bells of different sizes made to order. These she planned to put on the sheep and enjoy their music when the flock came in at night.

Having lost their only child, the Sills brought with them the son of a Congregational minister of Troy,

Richard Stowe, who also had ideas of being a rancher. Investing all their money in land near Guide Rock, they started the Sill and Stowe Sheep Ranch. The project was doomed from the beginning. Enthusiastic but un-informed, they imported blooded rams from Scotland and when the animals arrived, so eager were the Sills to get on with the business that they turned the rams in with the flock, with the result that all the lambs were born in winter and many of the ewes and lambs died. Frantically, the would-be ranchers rushed to Guide Rock and Red Cloud to buy nursing bottles. At one time they had seventy lambs in their great sod house, but in spite of all they could do, most of the flock died. Miss Cather used a similar incident in *One of Ours*.

About that time the Burlington Railroad was adver-tising Nebraska as a great sheep country. "If I could write all I know about sheep raising in Nebraska," laughed Mrs. Sill, "the Burlington would pay me so much to suppress it that I would be rich."

Her laughter over misfortune was characteristic. When their sod house burned and she lost all her lovely wedding gifts and many of her paintings, she shrugged her shoulders. Their sheep adventure over, the Sills sold their land and moved to Red Cloud where he made farm loans and she conducted classes in painting and music. Her painting group learned much more than just how to put color on canvas. While they worked, she read from classics or related her experiences abroad, and when she was correcting one student's work, she turned the reading over to whoever was free at the moment.

* * *

It was years later that Willa met another artist in Red Cloud. During one of her visits home, she and her father went to see the little Danish church which Yance Sorgensen, a Norwegian immigrant farmer, had built and decorated. He had hired a Czech named Ondrak to paint a picture above the altar. Ondrak had gone to art school at Prague and Munich, much against the wishes of his pharmacist father who wanted his son to follow him in the business. Eventually Ondrak drifted to America where he called himself a decorator. He had done some rather crude murals on the upper interior walls in some homes, but like many of his countrymen, he supported himself as a housepainter. His speech was broken, he walked with a limp, his clothes never matched; but he knew a great deal about the music and culture of the old country and he spoke excellent French. He seemed a dual personality, full of conflicts, and he spent a considerable amount of his time with hoboes. But Willa liked him and enjoyed talking with him.

The subject he had chosen for the painting in the church was "Christ in the Garden." When Mr. Cather saw it, he smiled and hesitatingly pointed out the crudities of the work. Willa was furious. "Father, you know you don't know a thing about art!"

"But," he protested mildly, "look at that halo. Just like a ring of cheese."

Willa would not agree. To her any sincere effort was worthy.

Later when a tornado destroyed the little church, Ondrak uttered the memorable cry: "My Yesus! My Yesus! Blown all to hell!" Ondrak lived in poverty for some years, and then not long before he died, inherited property from his father in Bohemia and was able to settle all his financial obligations.

When Willa went abroad in 1902 she had an opportunity to visit many galleries, but the place which impressed her the most—at least she used it for the setting and framework of the story "The Marriage of Phaedra" in *The Troll Garden,* was the Kensington Studio of Sir Edward Burne-Jones. She wrote feelingly of Burne-Jones' work, but perhaps she was most impressed with the devotion of his valet, caretaker of the studio in London.

After *O Pioneers,* Miss Cather realized that artists (in the narrow sense of those who paint pictures) and their lives were not her best materials, but she continued to admire and enjoy good work. In Europe she met Bakst, the Russian artist, who painted the portrait of her which now hangs in the Omaha Public Library. The two of them agreed on the subject of woman's dress, Bakst being one of the pioneer propagandists to change women's clothes from the corset era to one of comfort. He gave Willa a dressing gown which the Russian women of his native province had made him, and she had it made into just such a loose jacket as he admired.

Actually Bakst was a painter of background scenery for theaters and not at all a portrait painter, but Miss Cather liked him and he admired her—so that apparently they convinced themselves that he could do justice to her likeness. When the portrait was hung, Carrie Miner Sherwood went to see it, and with many others agreed that the portrait was so unlike her as to be almost unrecognizable. When Willa asked for an opinion, Mrs. Sherwood admired the rubber plant in the brass vase in the background.

Willa wrote back saying that if she ever had a good portrait made, she would give it to the Omaha Public Library, and Carrie could cut out the vase and rubber plant for herself.

Grant Reynard, Nebraska-born painter who in lecture tours around the United States never fails to acknowledge his debt to Miss Cather, recalls his first years of painting at the MacDowell Colony in Peterboro, New Hampshire, where Willa Cather was working on *Death Comes for the Archbishop*. He had come to the Colony to free himself from the drudgery of commercial art and, "with great canvases and material" felt that now he was really going to act like an artist and indeed had chosen "arty" subjects "like ladies and goats, nude ladies romping with the goats through the woods." Hearing that a countryman was in the neighborhood, Miss Cather had asked permission to call and see his work. Reynard recalls how she had, on arrival, completely ignored his "great paintings" and instead spent the entire time describing her own life, from her early youth in Nebraska to the glamour of her newly-found fame, her early writing and her few attempts at "fine writing." And she told how it wasn't until she "turned the carpet over and looking at the dusty back of it remembered the little Bohemian maid ('hired girls we called them') who had befriended her in her early youth out in Nebraska, and rolling the curtain back she wrote in a flood of feeling about those times and days."

She was convinced that the great thing was *desire* in art, that a desire to express ourselves be a clear compelling thing that must out, whether it be a poem, a painting, a novel, a symphony, or a piece of sculpture. . . . Our talk finished and she left me among the ruins of my goats and ladies, a bewildered young man if there ever was one.

[165]

If there is one thing that Miss Cather is better known for today than any other, it is her own economical artistry in the choice of her words. She would search months for the proper word, would never accept an unfamiliar one, and her final choice could seldom be bettered. When she and a friend were on the train going to Omaha where Miss Cather was to lecture, the author took her portfolio in hand but before she moved to another seat to study, she said, "I want you to look out on the cornfields and get me one word to describe the color of the corn. One word—not a hyphenated one. I've always called it blonde."

The track led along the Republican Valley through fertile farmland, rich in autumn harvest sunshine. Miss Cather's friend had painted a great deal and she saw at once that the corn was neither yellow nor tan. When Willa returned, the friend said, "Blonde is a better word than I can find; but if I were painting, the first paint I'd put on my pallette would be Naples yellow."

A few weeks later Willa wrote that she had read a story saying that the first man to use Naples yellow was Titian, and that when he was seeking new colors, he used the marble, crushed to powder, which had been soaking up sunshine for thousands of years.

V

"The Art of Living"

The old-fashioned farmer's wife is nearer to the type of the true artist and the prima donna than is the culture enthusiast.

Miss Cather held that artistic appreciation should include all the activities of life, from the enjoyment of the morning bath to cooking a roast just right, "so that it is brown and dripping and odorous and *saignant.*"

The farmer's wife who raises a large family and cooks for them and makes their clothes and keeps house and on the side runs a truck garden and a chicken farm and a canning establishment, and thoroughly enjoys doing it all, and doing it well, contributes more to art than all the culture clubs.

Most of the woman artists I have known—the prima donnas, novelists, poets, sculptors—have been women of this same type. The very best cooks I have ever known have been prima donnas. When I visited them the way to their hearts was the same as to the hearts of the pioneer rancher's wife in my childhood—I must eat a great deal, and enjoy it.

She criticized people who thought art something extraneous, to be "imported and tacked on to life," and found fault with young authors who started their stories with a few observations about the weather to add local color. She found the results "invariably false and hollow. . . . Art must spring out of the very stuff that life is made of."

The German housewife who sets before her family on Thanksgiving Day a perfectly roasted goose, is an artist. The farmer who goes out in the morning to harness his team, and pauses to admire the sunrise—he is an artist.

This is the type of heroine Miss Cather uses in *My Ántonia, O Pioneers* and *Shadows on the Rock.* Artists of this type abounded in Willa's background. One family, the Birkners, found their way into several of her books. Their mother spoke German. The children, although not scholars, had to Willa an innate fineness. They are the lads of *A Lost Lady* who would never betray her. Like "Adolph Blum" in that book, young Rhine Birkner, on the occasion that Carrie Miner Sherwood's mother died, appeared at the back door with a large box of roses, saying: "For your mother, from me and the boys."

DRAMA

I

"Man-eating Tiger"

WILLA CATHER was not an immigrant pioneer, yet she wrote *O Pioneers* and *My Ántonia*; she was not a Catholic, yet she wrote *Death Comes for the Archbishop* and *Shadows on the Rock*; she was not a musician, yet she wrote *Song of the Lark* and *Lucy Gayheart*. She was not a man yet she wrote two of her books and several of her stories from a masculine viewpoint. How was she able to do this? In 1915, long before Dr. Freud's discussions on vicarious identification became popular, she told H. W. Boynton of the "New York Evening Post":

I have never found any intellectual excitement more intense than I used to feel when I spent a morning with one of these pioneer women at her baking or buttermaking. I used to ride home in the most unreasonable state of excitement; I always felt as if they told me so much more than they said—as if I had got inside another

[169]

person's skin. If one begins that early, it is the story of the man-eating tiger over again—no other adventure ever carries one quite so far.

The fact is that Willa was always something of an actress. She once said that for those who live by the imagination, that part of their life is the only part that goes deep enough to leave any impression.

The first account we have of Willa's histrionic ambitions is recorded in the Red Cloud paper of May 14, 1885:

The Sunday School concert at the Baptist church Sunday Eve was of the usual high standard—Miss Willie Cather electrified the audience with her elocutionary powers.

and of June 11, 1885:

The recitation by Miss Willa Cather was particularly noticeable on account of its delivery which showed the little miss to be the possessor of extraordinary self-control and talent.

Willa was then eleven. One of her most popular selections was Hiawatha, during the recitation of which she held a bow and arrow and fell to one knee at the proper moment to shoot into the imaginary forest.

Willa was not a child who cared for dressing up dolls.

She would rather dress herself up and pretend. Her model and instructor in dramatic arts was Bess Seymore, a cousin who lived with the Cathers and who took the lead in the community plays. Usually rehearsals took place at the Cather home where Bess improvised costumes from Mrs. Cather's wardrobe, and where the large front room with adjacent hallway made an excellent stage. By the time Willa was thirteen, she was improvising and managing plays of her own. Many of them were not performed on even a makeshift stage: they were lived.

By that time she had read Robert Louis Stevenson and gave the landmarks along the Republican River such names as "Robber's Cave," "Dragon's Slide," and "Pirate's Island." She and her playmates hunted big-game—tadpoles to be carried home in tin pails, turtles and drowned-out gophers. Sometimes the dramas Willa enacted were so realistic that little Irene Miner, the youngest of the children, was not sure how much was fact and how much fancy. One evening at supper she recounted the horrible events of the day in such a realistic and excited manner that her father said: "I think the Miner children and the Cather children should be separated for a while or they'll all grow up to be inveterate liars."

In 1887 two events fanned the flame of Willa's dramatic fire. Dr. McKeeby, the Cather family doctor, was elected mayor of Red Cloud and Charles Cather, her father, alderman; and a contract was let for an iron bridge over the Republican River. The wooden ones floated away too easily in spring floods.

Thirteen-year-old Willa decided to be mayor of a town of her own—"Sandy Point." The town was constructed of packing boxes obtained from Miner Brothers' Store, and arranged along the south fence of the Cather yard, under the shade of cottonwood and wild plum. Willa persuaded her father to order half a dozen loads of sand and her brothers graveled a strip the entire length of the yard for "Main Street." Each child could choose his business and he was instructed to make an appropriate sign for his store.

Willa campaigned for mayor, but actually she had little opposition. Her only rival was Margie Miner who was content to be alderman. Of this period Irene Miner Weisz remembered: "There's no question about it. Willa started her literary career in Sandy Point. She was editor of our play paper, 'The Sandy Point News,' as well as mayor," and to Willa she said:

"Do you remember buying my vote with a sack of candy?"

"My only plunge into politics," laughed Miss Cather.

Willa established her office near the center of "Main Street" and began business by calling the citizens to discuss building a bridge over a ditch on the north side of

The sod house of the Henry Lambrecht family, lifelong friends of Willa's, was unique in that it had a cellar under it. This made it necessary to have a board floor—an almost unheard-of luxury in those early days.

The Boy's Home Hotel was described by Miss Cather in *My Ántonia* as the hotel run by Mr. and Mrs. Gardener. Complete with "sample rooms" for visiting traveling salesmen, it was first called Boy's Home, then Gardener House, later Holland House.

In the Paine homestead lived Alverna Cather Paine, Willa's aunt and the last
of the Cather sisters to die. The small trees planted around the yard were already
beginning to counteract some of the desolation of the prairie. The crop in the
background is probably broomcorn or sorghum, grown extensively in pioneer days.

Home from the University, Willa used to read to her youngest sister and brother, Elsie and Jack, in the Cather yard. Every Red Cloud home had a picket fence in those days to keep out stray stock that might wander in from the open range.

Willa gave a party in '31 for these children of the Red Cloud Episcopal Sunday School, grandchildren of old friends. Willa ran upstairs to hide from photographer until assured the man wasn't from a newspaper.

Willa's brother Douglas once worked at the Burlington Station in Cheyenne Wyoming. Willa went out to visit him and was photographed driving a handca along the right of way.

That same summer Willa, her friend Isabelle McClung and Douglas went on camping trip to Laramie with wagons and a guide, Old Ben, (center) whos wife, he said, had been to college. They later found he meant Barbers' College

the Cather yard—a worthy project in view of the fact
that Margie had been ill with infantile paralysis and
had to be pulled in a wagon. The children responded
very well. Willa's brothers, Roscoe and Douglas soon
had the bridge completed.

Sandy Point's fire department is credited with putting out a blaze in the Cather home when a new gaso-
line stove exploded. Other business enterprises were:
Margie Miner's store which kept tablets, pencils and
whistles; Jessica Cather's post office and Fair Store; Clara
Alden's piano-box hotel. Mary Miner had a candy shop,
for she was the only one who would and could make
taffy. Willa and Margie scorned domesticity and the
other girls were too young. Irene Miner and Laura
McNitt from next door kept a millinery shop which
was a two-story building. These girls were small enough
to climb into the upper box, and they thought the second floor gave privacy for trying on their hats.

The citizens of Sandy Point earned their own money
and bought their own supplies; but they accepted contributions such as would nowadays be sent to a rummage sale. In their civic transactions they used pins and
the Confederate bills which the Cather family had used
for packing dishes in the trip from Virginia.

But sometimes Willa would tire of so much confusion and she would retire to her upstairs room where
she discovered a knothole through which, on a hot day,

she could see across the lumber yard, east and along Crooked Creek, a mirage in which everything appeared upside down. She began to dream of directing her first play.

When cooler weather came, she dramatized a current story, "Dr. Allen," and the children presented it at the Miner home, where the entrance hall could be used as dressing room, the parlor as stage, and the dining room as auditorium. In the open arch between the parlor and the dining room, the girls fixed sliding curtains. "Dr. Allen" was a farce about psychiatry in which Mary Miner, the doctor, was supposed to diagnose and cure Willa, the eccentric patient. Besides the parents, the guests were Dr. and Mrs. McKeeby, Governor and Mrs. Garber, Mr. and Mrs. Wiener, Mr. and Mrs. Holland—all of whom were to appear later as characters in Willa's books.

The evening was such a complete success that the following year, 1888, when the blizzard left many people destitute, the children put on a play at the Opera House for charity—there being no organized help for the needy.

They enlisted expert assistance in the persons of Mrs. Sill and Will O'Brien, a clerk in Miners' Store. Mr. O'Brien had studied Shakespearian roles in Boston and New York, was an expert on speech and diction, and had already taught some of the children to dance. Mrs.

[174]

Sill, who was interested in all community activities, made an enthusiastic and resourceful coach. Mrs. Miner made the costumes.

The girls chose "Beauty and the Beast." All parts were to be spoken except certain soprano solos for Beauty—to be played by Margie Miner with her high sweet voice—and the choruses for the dancing fairies who wore filmy pastel garments. Margie began her performance in rags but triumphed in the last act in a delicate pink silk gown with train. Mary Miner, the Beast, was first dressed in a gray padded flannel suit with a mask made to simulate a bear's face. Carrie Miner, the stage manager, made up faces and transformed the Beast into a Prince in regal blue satin and velvet suit trimmed with silver. Willa, the merchant father, dressed herself in suit, hat, and waxed mustache.

The performance was a great success. When Mary came lumbering onto the stage chanting the weird melody and swaying to the rhythm of the Italian minstrels' bear dance, the atmosphere was so realistic that one nervous woman screamed. Mrs. Newhouse, a German woman who ran a local store, detained Carrie after the play: "Carrie, where did you get dat boy?"

Carrie laughed, "That wasn't a boy. That was Willie Cather."

The old lady shook her head. "Dat not Villie Cader.

He valk like boy. He talk like boy. Dat not Villie Cader." And she went away shaking her head.

The Red Cloud Daily "Evening Chief" for February 6, 1888 noted:

Willa Cather took the part of 'The Merchant' and carried it through with such grace and ease that she called forth the admiration of the entire audience. It was a difficult part and well-rendered.

The net proceeds of the play were $40.00 which was distributed in the form of groceries for needy families. That of Uncle Jerry, a local indigent Irishman, was typical. He would come to Carrie Miner, custodian of the funds, and say, "Indaid, and I'd like to have some more coffee."

"Why, Uncle Jerry, there were two pounds in your box last week."

"Do ye mind and Oi have me ten children and ivery one of 'em back to the least drinks his cup o' coffee?"

The next opportunity for dramatic talent came in the 1888 Fourth of July parade which was suggested and supervised by Mrs. Sill. There is no record that Willa took part in this parade. Her father was writing abstracts and was not in charge of any business house. But the following year, Willa paraded for Dr. Cook's pharmacy. Dressed in black velvet with a mantle and knee

[176]

pants, she was the ancient Alchemist. She wore, attached to her garments, a profusion of corn plasters, surgical instruments, tobacco and pipes, bottles of chemicals, and almost every article related to pharmacy.

Willa graduated from the Red Cloud High School in 1890, in a class of three, the second class to leave the school. Each of the three gave an oration. The Red Cloud "Chief," Friday, June 13, 1890 reported:

The oration of John Tulleys on 'Self Advertising' shows that John is one of our brightest young students and will make his way to fame . . . Alex Bentley followed with an oration on 'New Times Demand New Measures and New Men' . . . Alex is making rapid strides in the educational line and in years to come will show what close application to study in early childhood will do for those who improve the opportunity . . . Miss Willa Cather treated the audience to a fine oration on 'Superstition Vs. Investigation,' which was a masterpiece of oratory. The young lady handled the subject with that skill that showed at once her knowledge of and familiarity with both history and classics of ancient and modern times. Her line of thought was well carved out and a great surprise to her many friends . . .

The writer of the news item (the same one who had for three years been insulting Mr. Cather and the "Big Eight") seemed sure of the success of the boys but no prediction of fame was made for Willa, the girl of the

class. Excerpts from the speech made by John Tulleys
will show the sort of competition she had:

A man should blow his own trumpet and the louder
and longer he can blow the deeper impression he will
make and the trumpet he uses should be made of brass
and the more brass it contains and the more vigorously
it is blown the louder it will sound . . . Taking *by any
means* as a motto, a shrewd man will succeed in any
business. Take a man who has failed, he has failed simply because he is too honest and generous, he attends
church more than he attends to his business, he gives
to the churches and other institutions when he needs
all his capital in his business . . . To puff yourself up
is the advice practically given by every one (moralists
excluded) and although this way of putting yourself
forward is abused by moralists they are paid by the ones
who do not abuse it. Now and then you find a man who
likes to do his work well, but this is decidedly a mistake
on his part for while he is taking so much pains he
might be doing something more beneficial to him and
in this billsticking world, it would never do to be
idle. . . .

It is not difficult to imagine what Willa must have
thought of her fellow graduate and his philosophy.

Several years before her graduation from high school,
Willa began to play a continuous role that lasted into
her second year at the University. When her brother
Jim was born, her mother was too ill to comb Willa's

long curly hair, and the girl went to the barber shop and had it cut short. At the same time she was planning to become a surgeon and she wished to dress the part. She affected the character of a boy, wearing a jacket, a derby hat or a cap and a white shirt; and she carried a cane.

At the University people thought her independent and eccentric. When the Union Literary Society put on a play—possibly Willa was its author—she took the role of a man and shocked many people. One day as she was standing in line at "The Hesperian" office, the boy behind her, seeing only the haircut and the white shirt, put his hand on her shoulder. When she turned around and he recognized her, he was most apologetic. This was still the 1890's.

However, under the influence of new friends, she began to let her hair grow and we next hear of her appearing in a long, shapeless white robe, her hair piled on top of her head, chanting in a Greek chorus. After the Greek enthusiasm came a period in which she affected left-bank Bohemianism.

Shortly after she went to Pittsburgh in 1896, she attended a woman's club in which the topic of discussion was Carlyle. When the ladies asked her opinion, she rose and repeated from memory an essay she had written during her preparatory English courses. The women thought her oratory extemporaneous, and they were greatly impressed, to Willa's secret amusement and scorn. Many of the ladies made social calls on her and wasted so much of her time that she decided to cut that sort of activity out of her life, and even in later years hated to make speeches, or receive casual callers. If she knew a lecture had to be made, she was unable to settle down to anything else until it was over.

II

"The Passing Show"

WILLA'S CAREER as a critic began with her article on Carlyle. At the University of Nebraska her English teacher, Professor Ebenezer Hunt, assigned in February of 1891 a paper on "The Personal Characteristics of Thomas Paine, as judged from his Writing." Some of his more nervous friends, however, knowing what trouble such an assignment would make in an overwhelmingly religious community, asked him to change the subject. He allowed himself to be persuaded and changed the surname from Paine to Carlyle. Willa's essay was so unusual that the professor, without her knowledge, gave it to the editor of the Lincoln "State Journal" where it appeared on Sunday, March 1, 1891.

Many years later, speaking of that morning, Miss Cather said that seeing herself in print in a regular publication changed her from a doctor into a writer—for "what youth could be unaffected by the sight of himself in print?" Many times in her adult years she expressed her gratitude to Mr. Charles Gere, owner and editor of the "Journal" and to Mr. Will Owen Jones, the managing editor, both of whom let her follow her own bent and outgrow her youthful, high-flung style whose only virtue, she admitted, was honesty.

Here is a sentence in the 'high-flung' style—a sentence which Professor Hunt copied on the blackboard for all his students to read, and a sentence which some of Willa's surviving classmates can still repeat from memory:

Carlyle . . . Like the lone survivor of some extinct species, the last of the mammoths, tortured and harassed beyond all endurance by the smaller, though perhaps more perfectly organized offspring of the world's maturer years this great Titan son of her passionate youth, a youth of volcanoes, and earthquakes and great unsystematized forces, rushed off into the desert to suffer alone.

The editor of the "Journal" wrote of the Carlyle essay:

The article on 'Some Personal Characteristics of
Thomas Carlyle' which appears in this issue of the
'Journal' is original work from the literary department
of the University of Nebraska. The writer is a young
girl of sixteen years of age who comes from Webster
County. A careful reading will convince any student of
literature that it is a remarkable production, reflecting
not a little credit upon the author and the university.

Her second publication was an essay on Hamlet, published November 1 and 8 in the "Journal." By 1893
Willa was a regular contributor. She began her Sunday
column "One Way of Putting It" on November 5,
1893, and continued it until her graduation. It was two
newspaper columns in length and was given a place of
prominence on the editorial page along with Walt
Mason and other currently popular writers. She described characters from life and sometimes wrote fiction.
Some of her characters were her classmates and friends,
thinly disguised, and some of these victims took bitter
offense at having their peculiarities thus publicly exposed. Willa made some lasting enemies—apparently
without realizing at the moment that she was doing so.

Of this period of her life she said:

I really had to work to go through college. I was dramatic critic on the 'Lincoln State Journal' receiving
$1.00 a night for my work. On Sundays I had four col-
umns of trash in the paper. I got $4.00 for this.

The task of being dramatic critic suited Willa. She had always been interested in acting, and even when yet a child she had begged her parents to take her along to Omaha to hear Booth and Barrett; but her father had thought her request only a childish whim. However, she had always been a faithful attendant at all the performances in the Red Cloud Opera House. Of the winters during her childhood, Miss Cather wrote, Oct. 1929, to her old schoolmate of University days, Harvey Newbranch, the editor-in-chief of the Omaha "World-Herald":

Half a dozen times during each winter . . . a traveling stock company settled down at the local hotel and thrilled and entertained us for a week. . . .

That was a wonderful week for the children. The excitement began when the advance man came to town and posted the bills on the side of a barn, on the lumber yard fence, in the 'plate glass' windows of drug stores and grocery stores. My playmates and I used to stand for an hour after school studying every word on those posters; the names of the plays and the nights on which each would be given.

If the company arrived on the night train, when we were not at school, my chums and I always walked a good half mile to the depot . . . to see that train come in. Sometimes we pulled younger brothers or sisters along on a sled. We found it delightful to watch a theatrical company alight, pace the platform while their baggage was being sorted and then drive off—the men in the hotel bus, the women in the 'hack.' If by any chance one of the show ladies carried a little dog with a blanket on, that simply doubled our pleasure. Our next concern was to invent some plausible pretext, some errand that would take us to the hotel. Several of my dearest playmates had perpetual entry to the hotel because they were favorites of the very unusual and interesting woman who owned it But I, alas, had no such useful connection; so I never saw the leading lady breakfasting languidly at nine. Indeed, I never dared to go near the hotel while the theatrical people were there—I suppose because I wanted to go so much.

Children have about a hundred years of unlived life wound up in them and they want to be living some of it. . . . How the barking of the dogs behind the scenes (Uncle Tom's Cabin) used to make us catch our breath.

In Lincoln, now that she had the chance, Willa went to every play that came, and for the virulence of her criticism she became known and dreaded by actors all over the United States. She said of Walker Whiteside in "Richelieu":

The main fault in his acting seems to be that he acts too much. He declaims constantly and hisses an invitation to dinner as if it were a summons to the block. . . . He pitches the key of his work too low and the key of his voice too high. . . . Of Mr. Whiteside's leading lady little need be said, and that little is said in all charity and sympathy. She has missed her calling. Her faint we will try to forget, let us remember her as we last saw her in health. 'Richelieu' is a poor play; Mr. Whiteside is a poor actor, yet he can be borne; but 'Richelieu' and Whiteside together!

But Miss Cather could be equally extreme in admiration. Of Clara Morris in "Camille" she said:

To commend, even to speak of the great work done on the Lansing stage last night seems almost presumption. Better work has never been done by any actress in any country. Nothing can be more natural than nature, more lifelike than life. . . . To criticize the way in which Clara Morris dies in 'Camille' would be as impertinent as (to criticize) any real death. One can only say of perfection that it is perfect; we have no adjectives to go higher. . . . 'Camille' is an awful play. Clara Morris plays only awful plays. Her realism is terrible and relentless.

Willa didn't always get away with her dogmatic criticisms. On March 18 the "Journal" published an evaluation of Miss Cather's ideas about Clara Morris, by "Jane Archer" who was really Miss Sarah Harris, then editor of the Lincoln "Courier," the society paper for which Willa later worked.

Willa criticized John Philip Sousa for the type of program his band gave, saying he must have a low idea of taste of Lincoln audiences, but she herself had written only a few days before:

Indeed, the size of the audience was a fair sample of the Lincoln public that will flock to see 'The Spider and the Fly' and let a play like this ('A Duel of Hearts') greet an empty house. The Lincoln public has disgraced itself again but as it spends most of its time doing that in one way or another further remarks are needless.

She declared flatly in an article on a Mendelssohn concert that Mendelssohn was "weak, pitiably weak and childish." This criticism was answered with some acerbity by Mr. Gustav Menzendorf, a leading Lincoln teacher of violin and orchestra.

In an article on the popular Julia Marlowe, Miss Cather set forth a precept which she was to follow in her own life:

Miss Marlowe is honest and conscientious enough in her work, but she has not a particle of heart. . . . After all, the supreme virtue in art is soul, perhaps it is the only thing which gives art the right to be. . . . All prettiness for its own sake is trivial. . . .

And speaking of acting, although the words are just as applicable to writing:

An actor's imagination is his genius; it should be fed by whatever is best in science, letters, art. He should know how it felt to be an Egyptian sunning himself on the marble steps of the temple of Elephantine, how it felt to go up to the Acropolis on a blue spring morning in Athens, how it feels to be a thirsty Bowery boy, hesitating between a free lunch of pork and beans or corn bread and cabbage. He should know how to ascend the steps of a throne and how a peasant scrapes the mud from his wooden shoes. Potentially he should know all manners, all people, all good and all evil.

Her reputation as a journalist was growing. The same Red Cloud "Chief" which had pointedly omitted any great predictions for Willa when she graduated in 1894 hailed her as a "potent factor in the Journalistic sea of Nebraska." They referred to her as a literary "woman of distinction."

In 1895 she joined the staff of the "Courier" whose editor, Sarah Harris, felt her style was "brave and sweet and full of individuality." She predicted the day would come, "if the child heart faint not," when Willa's name would rank high in the annals of American Literature.

After her graduation in 1895, she continued working on the "Courier," then returned in the winter to Red Cloud where she remained until late June of '96 when she went to Pittsburgh to become editor of the "Home Monthly." She continued her critical writing there and

[1 8 7]

in her other positions on the "Daily Leader," "The Library," and much later, "McClures." At intervals she sent back contributions. The "Courier" kept printing her column "The Passing Show" from October 1897 to May 1900. The "Journal" ran a column from Washington, D.C., from Dec., 1900 to March, 1901. And when she went abroad in 1902, she sent back correspondence for the "Journal" from July to October.

From this trip one critical report is of interest in view of the fact that later Miss Cather spent some time in Ellen Terry's home and "ghosted" her autobiography.

Probably no play has been produced in London for some years which has proved so solid a financial success as Mr. Beerbohm Tree's revival of 'The Merry Wives of Windsor' . . . a means that at last brought about a truce between the two most popular women on the English stage—Mrs. Kendal and Ellen Terry. The spirit, the dash and gleam of the whole performance emanate from Ellen Terry. . . . Now I believe I understand better that wildfire wit which has always baffled me. There is a bit of old England left in Ellen Terry. . . .

III
"I Began by Imitating"

WHILE IN Red Cloud High School, Willa had helped edit the school notes for the Red Cloud "Chief." Her next editorial position at Lincoln, was shared by Louise Pound, later of the University of Nebraska English Department, and sister of Dean Roscoe Pound. The girls were associate editors of the "Lasso," a monthly student publication of the University. Willa was literary editor of the "Hesperian," another student publication, the year of 1892-3 and managing editor from 1893-4. As editor of the "Sombrero," the annual for the class of 1895, Willa rejected a story written by one of her best friends, Mariel Gere, entitled "How We Stole the Bust of Darwin. . . ."

The Botanical Seminary boys had bought a bust of Darwin to present to Professor Charles Edwin Bessey of the department of Botany; but that morning when Willa and Mariel went into the museum to see a newly-acquired mummy of a child, they noticed the bust and conceived the idea of hiding it. They wrapped it in charts and laid it on the top shelf of the dark room where, if anyone looked, he could see the white bulge

[189]

of Darwin's head. Then the girls told the janitor their secret and went on to classes.

In a few minutes someone rushed into the laboratory where Mariel was working and exclaimed, "Someone has stolen the bust of Darwin!"

"Have you looked in the Physics lab sink?" suggested Mariel, and chuckled as she heard footsteps clattering upstairs.

The girls had no idea that the bust would not be found in time for the presentation; but the hour came and passed. Finally Mariel wandered into the museum, looked toward the white bulge of Darwin's head, and soon others joined her. The bust was found.

The "Hesperian," claiming to know all about the "boy" who had stolen the bust, carried a warning notice; but the truth was never revealed. Willa exercised her editorial right of censorship.

Far greater responsibility than editing out a college prank fell to her on her next job, the managing editorship of the "Home Monthly" a magazine put out in Pittsburgh by Axtell, Orr & Co. Their purpose was to start a publication to compete with the "Ladies' Home Journal," and after friends had helped Willa get a job, Mr. Axtell went on a trip West and left her to run the whole show. She had to write half the first issue herself, and she claimed she used a half-dozen different pen-names. Moreover, the plant foreman was not accustomed to magazine work and Willa had to oversee everything in the composing room. Like many a young editor before and since, she was grateful for her experience on student papers.

Some nights she was up until one o'clock struggling over the forms and making up the magazine. She was entrusted with all manuscript reading and purchasing for the following number, and correspondence with authors. Her principal asset was a stenographer who could spell. The responsibility was so great that when she finally got to bed she dreamed about the magazine all night, but the job seemed like heaven after the depressing inactivity of Red Cloud. She enlisted friends in Lincoln to get her material on Mrs. William Jennings Bryan—she wanted to scoop the other magazines—and she went down to Canton, Ohio, to get information about Mrs. McKinley.

However, Willa was not altogether pleased with her magazine from a literary standpoint. The publishers wanted something that would appeal to the mass of people, and an article on "how children should care for their teeth" might receive much more attention than one of Willa's pieces of fiction. The sort of piece Willa wanted to write was too heavy for the magazine, and she rebelled at the "trashiness" of what she was compelled to use, but she decided that the idea was to work whether or not one was suited to it. Something in the challenge appealed to her, and she did her best to write home and fireside stuff.

There were compensations. She met many interesting people, but the one she considered the most stimulating—worth going to Pittsburgh for, if for nothing else—was Rudyard Kipling with whom, she told friends somewhat proudly, she spent forty-six minutes. Then too, she wrote a serial, "The Count of Crow's Nest," and showed it to one of her friends, a manuscript reader on "Cosmopolitan." He offered $100.00 for it, but she needed it for her own paper. Nevertheless, she was beginning to feel that she had come into her own intellectual country. She enjoyed the manuscript reading, and the proof reading was not too difficult. Now and then she took time off to write what she really wanted. The more she wrote, the more convinced she became that the "Home Monthly" was nothing more than a way to make a living, and a poor one at that.

About this time she began to foresee that the publication might not last forever, and she went to interview W. A. Magee, the man who once reputedly "owned Pittsburgh," to ask about writing for his two newspapers. He told her that for the time being, she might do some feature articles. By 1898, however, she was busy in the office of the "Daily Leader," rewriting war dispatches from Cuba, and headlines about Cervera's being bottled up in Santiago harbor.

She seems to have had the usual problems of reporters. Once she interviewed Harold Bauer, the pianist, for the paper but he talked so fast about Nietzsche that Willa couldn't understand him and had to call on her friend George Seibel to give her some facts on the subject. Later in New York she came to know Bauer much better.

Sometime in 1900 a new magazine, "The Library" was started and Willa wrote for it under several different by-lines. This magazine, however, was as short-lived as the "Home Monthly" and in 1901 Willa took a job as head of the English Department at Allegheny High School. She felt that journalism left her no time to write, and indeed the less hectic years between 1901 and 1906 saw the appearance of *April Twilights* and *The Troll Garden.*

The calm was not destined to last, and in 1906 Willa was again plunged into the publishing maelstrom, this time on the flourishing "McClure's." There are a number of legends concerning Willa's phenomenal ascent from the obscurity of the Pittsburgh school system to the managing editorship, in two short years, of what was at the time one of America's foremost popular monthly magazines. Some say one of Sam McClure's readers spotted an unsigned four-line poem of Willa's somewhere and told him "let's find the writer of that poem and get him in here!" Closer to the facts, probably, is the version that Willa sent the manuscript for *The Troll Garden* to McClure, who immediately wired her to come to New York for a conference. Whatever the details, however, McClure published *The Troll Garden* in book form, reprinting several stories from it in the magazine, and the next year offered Willa a job. Among her other assignments, she ghosted an autobiography for Mr. McClure himself, and completed the research and writing of a serialized and highly controversial "Life of Mary Baker Eddy," and from 1908 to 1912 held down the managing editorship.

The six years I spent on 'McClure's Magazine' in an editorial capacity, I call work. It was during the six years . . . that I came to have a definite idea about writing. In reading manuscripts submitted to me, I found that 95 percent of them were written for the sake of the writer—never for the sake of the material. The writer wanted to express his clever ideas, his wit, his observations.

Almost never, did I find a manuscript that was written because a writer loved his subject so much he had to write about it.

Usually when I did get such a manuscript it was so crude it was ineffective. Then I realized that one must have two things—strong enough to mate together without either killing the other—else one had better change his job. I learned that a man must have a technique and

[194]

a birthright to write—I do not know how else to express it. He must know his subject with an understanding that passes understanding—as the babe knows its own mother's breast.

*   *   *

In 1908 Willa had met Sarah Orne Jewett and Mrs. James T. Fields, both of whom Miss Cather remembered in *Not Under Forty*. Miss Jewett, then one of New England's most formidable authors, encouraged Willa and gave her advice on one of the stories Willa had had published in "McClure's," "On the Gull's Road," and cautioned her against using a masculine point of view, as Miss Cather had done in that story. Miss Jewett commended "The Sculptor's Funeral" as the best story in *The Troll Garden,* and regretted that Willa must spend so much time with her magazine job when she should be writing, pointing out to her that when one's first working power is spent, it cannot be regained, and that one needs quietness to perfect and mature one's talent. Willa was deeply influenced by Sarah Orne Jewett, but in at least two respects didn't follow her advice: she did not leave "McClure's" until financially able to do so in 1912, and in 1918 she returned to the masculine viewpoint with a vengeance to write her best book, *My Ántonia.*

IV

". . . And a Birthright to Write"

SO FAR AS WE KNOW Willa's first essay was about dogs. Written on an odd scrap of paper in an unformed, childish scrawl, it is apparently an argument for a debate, and extolls the virtues of dogs as opposed to cats. The spelling is Willa's, and amateur child psychiatrists are at liberty to draw their own conclusions:

The dog is a very intelligent animal. . . . The nature of most dogs is kind, noble and generous. O! how different from the snarling, spitting crul cat. . . . Newfoundland dogs are also famous for their way of saving the lives of people when drowning. And the St. Brenards are often trained in Switzerland to find travelers in the snow and carry them to a place of safety.

Pugs & Poodles are famous for nothing unless it is their expensive funerals which sometimes amont to one thousand dollers. Lord Byron, one of our greatest poets wrote a beautiful elegy on a dog, who ever wrote enything on a *Cat*? Did you ever see a tall massive dog with curly hair bright eyes and a knowing air? Did you ever see a poor thin scraggy cat, with dirty hair dull green eyes and drooping tail. If so I leave it to your common sense to awnser for I know you will say the noble majestic dog.

[196]

On a trip back to Virginia, Willa said she remembered it so well she knew just what lay ahead around the corner. Flyleaf dedication of Carrie Miner Sherwood's copy of O Pioneers (right) reads: "This was the first time I walked off on my own feet—everything before was half real and half an imitation of writers whom I admired. In this one I hit the home pasture and found that I was Yance Sorgeson and not Henry James."

After she joined the staff of "McClure's," where she soon became Managing editor, Willa appeared in this brown silk velvet dress with matching hat trimmed in gold and osprey feathers. The necklace was a gift from Sarah Orne Jewett. Made of white jade tinted with pink and green, it was something of a display piece in the days before jade became popular for jewelry.

Willa went on to applaud the sheep dogs of Virginia and dogdom in general, but at the bottom of the paper, above Grandfather William Cather's signature, is the single word: "Defeated."

Her next essay, as far as it is known, was her high school graduation oration, inscribed in a flowery language and peppered with classical allusions.

Willa's essay on Carlyle at the University of Nebraska gave rise to considerable comment. She admired Carlyle's half-dreaming attitude, his search for cause and effect, his indifference to society, his pleasure in living in the open air.

Nothing has so degraded modern literature as the desperate efforts of modern writers to captivate the public, then watching the variation of public taste as a speculator watches the markets. . . . He (Carlyle), himself, would suffer any privation rather than sacrifice an ideal; but for his brothers' sake he wrote for money. It seemed to him like selling his own soul . . . hacking his own flesh, bit by bit, to feed those he loved . . . proudly refusing a tomb in Westminster, as did one other great English writer, he was buried out on the wild Scotch heath, where the cold winds of the North Sea sing the chants of Ossian among the Druid pines. . . . He dreamed always—great, wild, maddening dreams: perhaps he sleeps quietly now—perhaps he wakes.

[197]

In October of 1892 she published in "The Hesperian" a story, "Lou, The Prophet," and in November of the same year, "Peter" which dealt with the suicide incident she used later in "Peter Sadelak, Father of Anton," in "The Library," and in *My Ántonia*.

Once during a summer vacation a Red Cloud boy was killed in a railroad accident east of town, and Willa went to the depot to meet the train which brought his body home. She heard comments to the effect that the boy "didn't amount to much anyway" and that "he was a cigarette fiend." Willa went to her room and wrote "The Night Express," a poem published in the 1903 *April Twilights* but left out of the later editions. More important, she used the same setting ten years later for "The Sculptor's Funeral," a short-story masterpiece and one of the most scathing denunciations of small-town smugness ever written in the English language.

Although her university years saw other fiction appear, it does not clearly point to the work she was to do later. In the "Sombrero" of 1895, Willa Cather and Dorothy Canfield collaborated on a prize-winning football story, a thriller in which the ghost of a dead player comes back to win the big game, largely by scaring the opposing team to death. Willa published several stories before her first important one, "Eric Hermannson's Soul," in "Cosmopolitan," in 1900. This story, later translated into German, was praised by a Dresden critic as a psychological masterpiece. In 1901 she wrote "Jack-a-boy," a story about her little brother published in the "Saturday Evening Post" and in 1902 she went abroad and absorbed some of the material she was to use in *April Twilights* and *The Troll Garden.*

The Troll Garden, 1905, was not a brilliant success and some of her Nebraska friends did not like it. A little bitterly, Miss Cather retorted:

They wanted me to write propaganda for the commercial club. . . .

An author is seldom sensitive except about his first volume. Any criticism of that hurts. Not criticism of its style—that only spurs one on to improve it. But the root-and-branch kind of attack is hard to forget. Nearly all very young authors write sad stories in revolt against everything. Humor, kindliness, tolerance come late.

From 1905 to 1913, Miss Cather was finding herself. Of *Alexander's Bridge,* 1912, she said later: "This was the only time I ever tried to be literary." The same year that *Alexander's Bridge* was published, Miss Cather also published in "McClure's" a story, "The Bohemian Girl," which was approaching more nearly the feeling of her next books, and when she left "McClure's" in 1912, she was capable of standing on her own feet. Of her work up to that time, she said: "I had been trying to sing a song that did not lie in my voice."

In order to understand a comment Miss Cather made about her work in *O Pioneers*, it is necessary to go back to the Norwegian settlement in Webster County where lived a bachelor named Yance Sorgensen. His older sister had come first to Council Bluffs, Iowa, and worked until she could pay passage for Yance. Then the two had saved until they could send for the mother, father and the others. Eventually, Yance had built up a huge estate which he named Norway Farm.

On several occasions Willa's father had suggested to Yance that he should modernize his home. "Why do you live like this? It's shameful for you to go without a bathroom and heat, and drive an open car when you could have the best of everything."

Yance had explained, "I'm so much more comfortable than I ever expected to be. When I first came here at nineteen, I had only my shirt and jeans. All winter I wrapped my legs and feet in paper and wound them with gunny sacks and herded cattle on the prairie." And not all the wealth Yance could ever acquire would cause him to change his original primitive ways.

When Miss Cather sent a gift copy of *O Pioneers* to Carrie Miner, she wrote on the fly-leaf:

This was the first time I walked off on my own feet— everything before was half real and half an imitation of writers whom I admired. In this one I hit the home pasture and found that I was Yance Sorgensen and not Henry James.

Willa had written O *Pioneers* to please herself. She wanted to tell the story of Alexandra Bergson and hardly thought it could be of interest to the reading public. When Ferris Greenslet of Houghton-Mifflin accepted it, no one was more surprised than she.

Her next book, *Song of the Lark*, did not completely suit her. She said that she had included too much material—had not stripped it thoroughly—and for that reason her English publisher turned it down. A precise and sparse style of writing—Willa called it the "novel démeublé" or "unfurnished novel"—later became the most easily identifiable trademark of Cather prose.

Before she wrote *My Ántonia*, she went into Burden's Store in Red Cloud and asked Mr. Jim Burden if he would do her a favor. "Why yes, Miss Willa. If I can."

"Would you mind if I used your name in my next book?"

"Why no. It would make me very happy."

Thus the name of Jim Burden was chosen for the narrator of *My Ántonia*, but the story is Willa's own, and in many ways is autobiographical. She didn't invent or contrive. "You can't write imaginary things. To have universal appeal, they must be true!"

Miss Cather's international success, after the publication of *O Pioneers,* was assured. Translations of her books were made into Czech, French, German and Norwegian until the work became a burden and she complained that her old books were preventing her from writing new ones.

In 1922 she won the Pulitzer Prize for *One of Ours;* in 1931, the Prix Femina Américaine for *Shadows on the Rock.* When Sinclair Lewis received the Nobel Prize in 1930, he was reported to have said that Miss Cather should have had it. Some of Miss Cather's Red Cloud friends, in bitter moments, felt that perhaps the Europeans could more easily interpret Mr. Lewis' books as discrediting the American way of life, and that they were happy to do so.

In 1934, Miss Cather was the only author with four books on the White House shelves. She was the first woman ever to receive an honorary degree from Princeton, and she received honorary degrees from the Universities of Nebraska, California, Columbia, Yale, Smith, Creighton, and Michigan. She was elected in 1938 to the American Academy of Arts and Letters; she won a Mark Twain award, but was too ill to attend the ceremonies. In 1944 she received a gold medal from the National Institute of Arts and Letters.

In 1920 Miss Cather chose Alfred Knopf as her publisher, and their relationship remained highly satisfactory until her death on April 24, 1947. She was one author who never asked for an advance—she had built up her own income so that she need be dependent on no one. Miss Cather paid tribute to Mr. and Mrs. Knopf on the twenty-fifth anniversary of the Publishing House, expressing her admiration for his individuality and leadership in choosing books for their value instead of their prospects as best sellers.

My Ántonia won Miss Cather acclamation both in the United States and Europe. Dr. Edward Benes of Czechoslovakia wrote her his appreciation of her interpretation of the Czech in America. In 1938, on the twentieth anniversary of the publication of *My Ántonia*, Miss Cather said:

The best thing I've done is *My Ántonia*. I feel I've made a contribution to American letters with that book.

V

"The Road is All"

WHILE WILLA CATHER was attending the University of Nebraska, she read and admired the great masters of prose style, particularly Henry James, whom she considered "the most interesting writer of that time." She began by imitating James, and it was not until she wrote *O Pioneers* that she stepped out into a style admittedly her own.

At the University Miss Cather disagreed strongly with certain policies of the English Department. She felt their method too analytical, their tearing apart of the classics in an attempt to find their basic formulae too brutal. She had frequent altercations with Dr. Lucius Sherman, head of the Department, who told her and others that with the course she was pursuing she would never get anywhere.

Encouraging Willa, on her side of the argument, was Herbert Bates, who had come from New England in 1891 and until 1897, when he returned East, did much to influence creative writing at the University. A tall, thin Episcopalian, ungainly and sarcastic, he inspired in his students either great admiration or intense dislike. His hobby was sailing on the artificial salt lake near Lincoln, and his first love poetry. He was largely the prototype for "Gaston Cleric" in *My Ántonia*, and one of the potent influences in Miss Cather's early poetry. During his stay at Lincoln he brought out a book, "Songs in Exile," in which he painted on the same canvas New England and the prairie, and described with fervent emotion the Nebraska plains.

Two other men besides Bates understood and helped

Willa. They were Ebenezer Hunt, who was instrumental in getting her first essay published in the "State Journal," and Will Owen Jones, journalism professor and later editor of the "Journal," who helped Willa get her job on that paper.

And during this period she met a living inspiration in the person of Stephen Crane. In the Spring of 1894, a slender, shabbily-dressed fellow sauntered into the office of the managing editor of the "State Journal" where Willa was working. As soon as she heard the stranger introduce himself, she dropped into a chair back of the editor's desk where she could listen without intruding. With her prairie background bounded on the one side by red grass, horses and cattle and on the other by the Greek and Latin classics she had read, she had come to the conclusion that nothing was of importance except good stories and the people who wrote them. This was the first genuine man of letters she had ever seen.

She cut classes to lie in wait for him, to catch him in some unguarded moment to discover from him the secrets which she was sure he held. She told herself that if "one burned incense long enough, the oracle would not be dumb." She was particularly eager to get his opinion of Maupassant, the current idol of her junior-year studies. But Crane only laughed at her, accused her, with a bad pun, of "Moping" and went on reading a volume of Poe which he carried with him.

She would not be discouraged. When she asked him if stories were constructed from mystical formulae, he sighed and shook his tired shoulders. "Where did you get all that rot? Yarns aren't done by mathematics. You can't do it by rule any more than you can dance by rule. You have to have the itch of the thing in your fingers, and if you haven't,—well, you're damned lucky, and you'll live long and prosper, that's all." And yawning, he walked away.

But at last the oracle spoke, and the revelation came. About eleven o'clock, on his last night in Lincoln, after Willa had come in from the theater to write her criticism of that evening's play, Crane showed up. He had been waiting for some money on the night mail, and it had not come. He was irritated and depressed. He sat on the sill of the open window facing on the street, listening to the gurgle of the saltwater fountain in the Post Office square and the tinkle of banjos from the Hotel Lincoln, where Negro waiters were entertaining the guests.

The night was oppressive, with a parching wind, characteristic of Nebraska, blowing up from the South. The streets were deserted; even the drop lights in the office behind him shed a dull gloom, and the telegraph bug ticked faintly away in the next room. As soon as

Willa had finished her piece she went over and took a chair beside Crane. Almost immediately he began to pour maledictions upon his trade, cursing it from the first beat of creative desire to the finished masterpiece. Although he did not raise his voice, he revealed in a slow, deadly monotone all the frustrations and bitterness of his life. He admitted that he was forced into leading a double literary existence—on the one hand writing slowly and critically, which pleased him, and on the other grinding out any sort of piece which would sell. He knew that the latter was as bad as it could be, but he also knew that he could not remedy the situation, that what he couldn't do, he couldn't do at all. . . . "I only hold one trump." That trump was talent.

What interested Willa most of all was the discussion of his slow method of composition. There was, he declared, little money in story-writing and particularly was this true of his work because of the length of time it took him to work up detail. Although he had written "The Red Badge of Courage" in nine days, he said that he had been unconsciously working it out ever since he could remember. His ancestors had been soldiers, and he had from childhood imagined countless scenes and campaigns. But on new material his imagination was "hidebound" and pulled hard, and even after he got the initial idea, he spent months getting any personal contact with it, or a feeling for the story. "The detail of a thing has to filter through my blood, and then it comes out like a native product, but it takes forever." Willa liked that idea. She was something like that herself.

*   *   *

Years later, after she had achieved success, she did not as a rule discuss her art, but while she was at the height of her fame, in July of 1922, she gave a series of lectures on writing at the Bread Loaf School of English, in Middlebury, Vermont. The talks were highly personal, and concerned her theory of writing, and the Dean of the School, Wilfred E. Davison, had a rule that no one was to take notes during the lecture, his idea being that the speaker would be inhibited if she saw her audience doing so. No record remains except in the memory of those who attended. They recall that her theory was not that writing was simple self-expression, but that the writer must be so in love with his subject that he forgets "self" in his passion. The intellect becomes the brake, the idea the power. Miss Cather told students that her first teacher in narrative was an old mountain woman in the hills of Virginia—very likely the mother of Margie who came to Nebraska with the Cathers—a woman who could neither read nor write, but who knew the life of the mountain, the folk phrases which no one had written nor could write, but which are the product of years and generations.

From time to time, too, Miss Cather would express some of her ideas on writing in interviews. In these, she readily admitted that writing was hard work, but work which she enjoyed as a tennis player might enjoy working his game from the commonplace into the smooth and expert. If one loved the work enough, it wasn't really work. Not that there wasn't a struggle in attempting perfection, but the struggle was one which stimulated. She compared the writer to the musician, writing being to the author what music is to the violinist. Many people, she said, have a little vocation, but there are those with a great vocation—men like Heifetz, whose vocation was his great potential.

When Miss Cather was in New York she worked nearly every day, writing first in longhand and then typing the second and third copies. Then she sent the manuscript to her typist, made corrections, and finally turned it over to her publishers. She disciplined herself to a schedule, which meant regular and early rising, a good amount of work each morning, with an afternoon free for study, recreation or rest.

When people ask me if it has been a hard or easy road (she once said) I always answer with the quotation, 'The end is nothing, the road is all.' The cups mean nothing to the tennis champions. I keep referring to tennis because it is the most sportsmanlike sport we have. It is the one game you can't play for money. That is what I mean when I say my writing has been a pleasure. I have never faced the typewriter with the thought that one more chore had to be done.

Miss Cather held no brief for schools and courses in short-story writing. She felt that they could only teach what others had already done, and if one wished to be original, he would have to find the way by himself.

My Ántonia, for instance, is just the other side of the rug, the pattern that is supposed not to count in a story. In it there is no love affair, no courtship, no marriage, no broken heart, no struggle for success. I knew I'd ruin my material if I put it in the usual fictional pattern. I just used it the way I thought absolutely true.

A school might teach the mechanical technique of fiction, and perhaps a "born artist" might not be harmed by the process any more than a talented violinist might be ruined by a period of playing in cabarets. In Miss Cather's opinion, "you can't kill an artist any more than you can make one." But, she pointed out, such ordinary attributes as health and will-power were essential. One must have enough vitality and stability to experience and feel life, yet he must not be drawn aside into all the pitfalls which admirers in his first flush of success might

open for him—the wining, dining and time-consuming
adulation of a new celebrity.

She didn't believe in "collecting ideas to build a
story." What the "born artist" gets is an emotion that he
wants to put into a design. "It reacts on him exactly as
food makes a hungry person want to eat. It may tease
him for years until he gets the right form for the emotion." A writer of little talent might have to be continually on the look-out for ideas—even the elder Dumas
used this method—but in such writing the situation
counts for a great deal. In Miss Cather's stories, the
characters and emotions are predominant.

The type of writer we have been talking about has a
brain like Limbo, full of ghosts, for which he has always tried to find bodies. *A Lost Lady* was a beautiful
ghost in my mind for twenty years before it came together as a possible subject for presentation. All the
lovely emotions that one has had some day appear with
bodies, and it isn't as if one found ideas suddenly. Before this the memories of these experiences and emotions have been like a perfume.

A writer's own interest in the story is the gauge which
measures the amount of warmth which will repeat itself
in the reader. This emotion she found "bigger than
style."

To me the one important thing is never to kill the figure that you care for, for the sake of atmosphere, well-balanced structure, or neat presentation. If you gave me a thousand dollars for every structural fault in *My Antonia* you'd make me very rich. I know they are there, and made them knowingly, but that was the way I could best get my squint at her. With those faults I did better than if I had brought them together into a more perfect structure. Sometimes too much symmetry kills things.

She once explained to a friend how a story started. First she felt it in the front of her head, where it enlarged as a baby grows in its mother's womb. And finally, it reached the back of the head where it lay heavy and painful awaiting delivery. Then she would be obsessed by the fear that something would prevent her bringing it to life.

"This One Thing I Do"

"No man can give himself heart and soul to one thing while in the back of his mind he cherishes a desire, a secret hope for something different."

WILLA CATHER'S LIFE seems to have been largely ruled by a oneness of purpose that exemplifies the above statement. When she went to the University of Nebraska in the fall of 1890, she immediately made friends with some of the "best" people of Lincoln, but she let neither her social life nor her school life interfere with her desire to attend all the plays, concerts and operas she could.

As a child in Virginia, Willa had gone to school just to sit and listen. Grandmother Boak had taught her to read and write. When the family first moved to Red Cloud, Willa didn't like her teacher and would not attend school. In fact, her total attendance before she went to the University amounted to not more than two years, and she was forced to spend a year in the preparatory class of the University before entering as a freshman. The selection of her subjects had been erratic. She knew literature, and the classics, but she knew nothing about mathematics. As she said later, "I'm a graduate of the University of Nebraska but I can't say the multiplication tables!"

When she began struggling with mathematics she reproached her father for not having compelled her to learn some elementary arithmetic. In fact, Willa did not get her college mathematics "incompletes" worked off until just before she graduated. After that, whenever she went to sleep exhausted, she would have guilty nightmares about not passing her examinations and not being able to get her diploma.

At the University she displayed the same independence that she had as a child. If she didn't like a teacher or his methods, she wouldn't attend his classes. But this attitude was no longer a frivolous whim of childhood. She had, even at this early date, made up her mind firmly that writing was to be her whole life, and justified her behavior in a newspaper column she wrote at the beginning of her Senior year:

The further the world advances the more it becomes evident that an author's only safe course is to cling to the skirts of his art, forsaking all others, and keep unto her as long as they two shall live. An artist should not be vexed by human hobbies or human follies; he should be able to lift himself into the clear firmament of creation where the world is not. He should be among men but not of them, in the world but not of the world.

Other men may think and believe and argue, but he must create.

After she became famous and the University of Nebraska talked of giving her an honorary degree, one of her former professors said, "Over my dead body!" She got the degree, and the spokesman remained alive and healthy.

At Lincoln she roomed at the home of "Aunt Kate Hastings" a friend of the family, where she had to tend her own stove—something she had never done before—and sweep her own floor, an imposition for which she compensated, according to friends, by "lifting the rug and sweeping the dirt under it." She boarded at the best eating place in town. Expenses in those days were moderate. One could get both board and room for less than fifteen dollars a month and University fees consisted of a ten dollar registration, good for the four years, and a ten dollar Chemistry fee which, minus breakage, was refunded at the end of the course. Although she would in later years hold forth about her poverty-stricken college career, Willa did not have to make her own way, nor did she very seriously suffer from a lack of the necessities of life. But her standards were so high that she felt it was important for her to see and do everything immediately. What she wanted then she wanted desperately, whether it was a dash to Omaha for a play, a trip to Chicago for the Opera, new clothes, photographs of herself wearing them, or books. Many of her friends were so well-off that she may, by comparison, have felt herself pinched. Then too, she loaned money to her newly-acquired actress friends whom she met through her drama critic's job on the "Journal," and they were not always too diligent about repaying.

She was extremely independent in dress and manner. First of all, she wore her hair cut in a boyish fashion. She worked on a newspaper and, after a late night's work, used to go into Harley's Drug Store for a soda. She was thought odd for all this, but outrightly criticized for her friendships with Dr. Tyndale and other gentlemen of the college community.

She had, however, loyal supporters against the critics and gossips, among them the Gere family, whose three daughters visited at the Cather home in the summer of 1893. It was Mrs. Gere who saw through Willa's self-imposed disguise. Mariel Gere told her mother that she wanted to bring home a girl who was sort of masculine. When Mrs. Gere had met Willa, she told Mariel, "She's not at all masculine." Before long, Mrs. Gere had persuaded Willa to let her hair grow, and she was wearing white blouses, skirts, and when she went to the theater, long white gloves.

Willa was not particularly anti-sorority at school, although she felt that a great deal of time could be wasted in such organizations. She and several other girls were going to organize a chapter at one time, but through lack of interest the plans fell through.

Like everyone else, she had her moments of discouragement and sometimes wondered if it were worth while going on to graduate. Among those who encouraged her was Evangeline King-Case, who had been her favorite teacher in the Red Cloud schools. Later Mrs. Case was superintendent of Webster County Schools, then of Red Cloud Schools, and eventually a teacher at Kearney State Teachers' College, where a hall is named for her. She is the "Evangeline Knightly" of "The Best Years."

The worst period of depression for Willa came after her graduation from college, a period of enforced vegetation at home. Her future seemed hopeless; she felt that everyone expected something special of her, but that she could never come through. She wrote to friends that she was too inexperienced, that her life had been too superficial. She even hated to work on her manuscripts. But she was delighted when she found someone who talked her language, and when she met a Miss Gayhardt while visiting friends at nearby Blue Hill, the two of them talked all night about the classics and French literature. On her return to Red Cloud the depression closed in worse than ever.

Another thing bothered Willa intensely. She had no

money, and the actresses who had to have their paste diamonds and champagne, while she lived in exile, hadn't paid up. She supposed that she was learning by experience, but felt she couldn't afford it right then.

Perhaps some of her theatrical friends paid part of their debt by putting in a good word for her in Pittsburgh. In any case, her exile soon ended in her trip there, and she afterwards referred to this city as the birthplace of her writing. She was happier there than she had been anywhere else since she left home. As she wrote friends, there was no short hair-cut, no Dr. Tyndale, no dramatic ambitions, nothing to queer things for her. And she quoted from Charles Lamb: "Gad, how we like to be liked!"

As a teacher of Latin and English, she was well-liked by her students for her inspiring, breezy Western way. She dressed plainly in tailored clothes with her hair parted in the middle like a madonna. "Paul's Case," one of her most famous short stories, is a composite of two tragic experiences from Willa's teaching years. The story followed a familiar Cather theme—the defeat of a young artistic temperament by a materialistic world.

Her pleasures in Pittsburgh were characteristically unconventional. She raced the electric cars on her bicycle and told friends she expected to get killed doing it. She went on excursions on the river, and once missed her regular reading of French with the Seibels to attend

a picnic of the glass-blower's union with the Labor editor of the "Leader."

Willa had had several admirers at the University,
and in Pittsburgh a young doctor wanted to marry her.
She admitted that it was a good match, but she did not
really care for him. Perhaps the real reason was that she
loved her freedom—her liberty to do exactly as she
pleased. She wanted nothing closer than friendship. As
she had said in her essay on Carlyle:

Art of every kind is an exacting master, more so even
than Jehovah—He says only, 'Thou shalt have no other
gods before me.' Art, Science and Letters cry, 'Thou
shalt have no other gods at all.' They accept only human sacrifices.

This was Willa's religion and she told friends she was
going to devote her life to the worship of Art and would
probably follow her creed to a place much hotter than
Pittsburgh. At this stage she did not hope for great creative success, but she meant to do her best, and if she
did her best and failed, she thought she could accept
that too. She compared herself to one who has taken
the veil—so absorbed was she in her work, and such
was her temperament that she enjoyed the isolation. It
was the beginning of that withdrawal which was later
to make her a recluse. She was already looking back on
her college days as the golden era of her life.

[219]

Miss Cather did not offer her own choice to remain single as a criterion for others. She said:

As for the choice between a woman's home and her career, is there any reason why she cannot have both? In France the business is regarded as a family affair. It is taken for granted that Madame will be the business partner of her husband; his bookkeeper, cashier, or whatever she fits best. Yet the French women are famous housekeepers and their children do not suffer for lack of care.

The situation is similar if the woman's business is art. Her family life will be a help rather than a hindrance to her; and if she has a quarter of the vitality of her prototype on the farm she will be able to fulfill the claims of both.

Yet there is evidence that Miss Cather's own sentiments were more like those of Mr. Keats's, in his "Ode on a Grecian Urn."

After all, it is the little things that really matter most, the unfinished things, the things that never quite come to birth. Sometimes a man's wedding day is the happiest day in his life; but usually he likes most of all to look back upon some quite simple, quite uneventful day when nothing in particular happened but all the world seemed touched with gold. Some times it is a man's wife who sums up to him his ideal of all that a woman can be; but how often it is some girl whom he scarcely knows, whose beauty and kindliness have caught at his imagination without cloying it!

Could it be that she avoided reaching out to grasp anything that might conceivably have vanished for her in the grasping? That she did not choose to marry does not mean that Miss Cather was incapable of deep emotional attachment. Rather, hers was a positive and joyous nature, and her reaction to people was violent—stormy as the tempests she so much enjoyed at sea or the winds that swept the Nebraska plains. For those she loved, her feeling was so intense that she would tremble at parting. She did not want people to come physically close to her unless she willed it, but she could be impulsive and capricious, as when at a meeting of the National Institute of Arts and Letters, she saw her old friend and employer Samuel McClure helped to the platform to receive a special award and rushed forward to kiss him.

If she met people with whom she had no sympathy she was revolted and she made no pretense to the contrary. Stories are told of her vitriolic treatment of those who annoyed her. As one newspaper reporter said, she built a battery of guns around her and it was rough going until you got inside the battlements, then everything was lovely. But some people could never get inside, and if a person Willa disliked were in the vicinity, she could scarcely endure it—pacing the floor, stamping her foot, and repeating the offender's name with bitterness.

There had been ample incidents for provocation. When Miss Cather was looking up material for *Death Comes for the Archbishop* in Denver, she did not want to be disturbed and took great care that no one should know she was in town. After she had gone, one of the Denver papers, having learned of her visit, published a story saying she had been there to have her face lifted —her reason for remaining incognito.

She particularly detested candid camera fans, until finally she hated the idea of photography in general. When someone wrote asking for the use of her picture to put on a calendar to be distributed at Christmas Time, her disgust was devastating, and she was unable to work all that day. Like many famous writers, she seemed to forget that she had once been a reporter, dependent on brashness and interference with privacy for news, and that there had been a time when she herself had needed and wanted publicity.

In 1931, when she was in Red Cloud for Christmas, she arranged her crèche and told the Christmas story to a group of children. One of Willa's friends had asked a photographer to come because she wanted a picture for each of the children; but when Willa saw the camera, she ran upstairs and refused to come down. Her friend found her crouched with her arm over her face as if expecting a blow; but when she was assured that the man wasn't from a newspaper, she came down.

When her publisher asked her to go on a lecture tour, she finally agreed, but she insisted on someone's sleeping in the outer hall of her suite to keep people away. When she spoke in Chicago, Irene Miner Weisz went with her, but the chairman of the program pushed Mrs. Weisz away saying, "You'll have to stay down here. There's a special place for Miss Cather on the stage."

Willa reached back and took her friend's hand. "Don't go any farther away, Irene. Stay close enough so I can hold your hand." Imperiously she turned to the woman in charge. "Get a chair for my friend and also a chair for the coats she is carrying."

When the lecture was over, the crowds were so great that Mrs. Weisz's chauffeur couldn't get to the front entrance, and sent word for them to come to the side door. As he pulled the long car into the alley, Miss Cather ordered the car to stop and called to several young girls with notebooks in their hands. "Were you girls at the lecture?"

They nodded.

"Then you know I'm Willa Cather."

The girls said yes.

"Do any of you collect autographs?"

They hurried to open their notebooks. Graciously she wrote a few lines and her name.

Once she offered to autograph a book for an old couple in a Red Cloud store. They thanked her, but said that since they were giving it as a gift, they didn't want anyone to think it was second-hand.

Miss Cather, about five feet, three inches tall, of a stocky build, with short neck, held her head high and squared her shoulders when she wanted to make a point. She liked to work in loose, comfortable garments, and clung to the skirt and shirtwaist style. Her street clothes were tailored, modest, and expensive. In her evening clothes she indulged her great love of color—bright green and any shade of red. They all suited her. She always wore low shoes and had her dress shoes made to match her costumes.

On the whole she was not overwhelmingly interested in clothes nor preoccupied about being stylish. Sometimes her close women friends would select her gowns, a thoughtfulness that Miss Cather appreciated.

She was an indifferent traveler, sometimes losing her purse or other of the many parcels she carried. When she came West, she always brought a trunkful of evening clothes for possible stopover, but in Red Cloud, she would dress up only for a few intimate friends.

Her withdrawal from public life was not without precedents. Gossip represented Hawthorne as inaccessible to invitations—as a recluse who would hurdle a fence and take to the fields to avoid a stranger on the road. Proust, whom Miss Cather admired, lived for years in complete isolation. Carlyle was fanatical about noise. Miss Cather, when she was living on Bank Street in Manhattan, rented the apartment above her own in order that she might keep it vacant and silent. In her will Miss Cather specifies that no letters of hers may ever be quoted—an attitude reminiscent of Henry James, who made a great bonfire of many of his personal papers, so that they might not be "at the mercy of any accidents."

*   *   *

Miss Cather said: "A book is made with one's own flesh and blood of years. It is cremated youth. It is all yours—no one gave it to you."

She contended that she had only a certain number of stories to write, a certain amount of cremated youth, and when she had done these, she would be written out. Others might have their professions and talents: her "only assets" were her stories. Perhaps in this lies an explanation for her withdrawal. As she burned herself away in her writing, she had less and less to give; and she did not have that saving sense of humor which has from the beginning of time enabled others to laugh at themselves. Her religion of Art she took very seriously.

[225]

In her choice of a final resting place, Jaffrey, New Hampshire, she may have been influenced by the fact that she had spent pleasant hours there, in a little room on the third floor of the Shattuck Inn, looking out toward Mt. Monadnock. (Or is it possible that when she thought of returning to Red Cloud she remembered the callous reception accorded her dead hero in "The Sculptor's Funeral"?) But when friends in Jaffrey lost a child, Miss Cather attended the funeral and was moved by the quiet and peace of the ancient, fern-covered burial place, from which one could look across to the mountain. Perhaps she had always wished to meet Death on a hilltop like "Myra Henshawe" in *My Mortal Enemy*. In her University days she wrote:

I hadn't been there long [Brownville, an old town on the Missouri] before I understood the feelings of the old Indian chief who when he lay dying asked for Governor Furnas and asked him to bury him high up on the bluff, sitting upright in his chair, with his face to the East so he could see the sun rise and watch the steamboats go up and down the river.

Of Miss Cather might be said, in paraphrase of the words she wrote of Carlyle: Throughout life . . . she dreamed always—great, wild, maddening dreams; perhaps she sleeps quietly now—perhaps she wakes!

THE WORLD OF WILLA CATHER

By Mildred R. Bennett

THE MOST APPEALING thing about this book is the widely varied and very human people which it re-creates and, through them, the little prairie town of Red Cloud. The group is so small and its living together so intimate that it becomes almost like a family, at least in its feeling about its most talented member who went out to become one of the great literary figures of the world.

These people were proud of her and yet she always remained to them, and still is today, a member of the family.

As this story so simply and naturally shows, the characters of Willa Cather's novels were taken from the people who lived around her and whom she knew so well. Though she lived in many other places after her girlhood, her creative imagination was always bound to that Nebraska countryside. Out of its courage, its rare beauty, its devotion and patience, its loneliness and toil, she fashioned, with her worldly genius, the greatness of her immortal books.

It is these actualities, the raw materials of Willa Cather's art, about which Mrs. Bennett has written. So well has she done it and so charming are these people that you would find this a most enjoyable book, even if you had never heard of its delightful presiding personality, Willa Cather herself.

The book contains a most interesting selection of photographs—24 of them—very few of which have ever been published previously.

WEBSTER STREET